Special Catholic Edition

Why
Wait
Till
Marriage

?

by Evelyn Millis Duvall
Ph.D.

Author of "Love and the Facts of Life"

Association Press, New York City

Why Wait Till Marriage?

Paperback Edition
Published in January, 1968

Copyright © 1965 by National Board of
Young Men's Christian Associations
Association Press
291 Broadway
New York, N. Y. 10007

Library of Congress catalog card number: 65-27834
Publisher's title stock number: 1670p

Cloth Bound Edition

FIRST PRINTING AUGUST, 1965

SECOND PRINTING NOVEMBER, 1965

NIHIL OBSTAT:	Richard A. McCormick, S.J.
	Censor Deputatus
IMPRIMATUR:	Most Rev. Cletus F. O'Donnell, J.C.D.
	Administrator, Archdiocese of Chicago
DATE:	June 22, 1965

*The Nihil Obstat and Imprimatur are official declarations that a book
or pamphlet is free of doctrinal or moral error. No implication is con-
tained therein that those who have granted the Nihil Obstat and Imprimatur agree with the contents, opinions, or statements expressed.*

Introduction

In search of an adequate recommendation for so valuable a book as this, I can only express the hope that it will be accepted in Catholic no less than non-Catholic circles on a par with the late Fr. Gerald Kelly's *Modern Youth and Chastity*. Dr. Evelyn Millis Duvall, from the wealth of a lifetime of lecturing and writing on youth and preparation for marriage, here presents in frank and specific language the reasons for premarital chastity.

She demolishes the popular fallacies concerning sex before marriage, never resting on the purely authoritarian approach. At the same time she constantly shows the reasonableness behind the religious authority for premarital chastity.

While addressed to teen-age readers, this book also holds all the answers for the harassed student counselor or teacher who looks for some successful method to cope with the glittering fallacies of the sensationally headlined announcements of approaching sexual freedom for all. The accurate descriptions of male and female psychological reactions to premarital sexual relations are priceless.

In a certain sense, this book should not be recommended primarily for the teen-age reader, if this would mean that parents were unaware of its contents. Too many parents of our day have fallen prey to the baseless claim that their sons and daughters must have early social dating, lest the children's social and emotional development be thwarted. Such parents are practically forcing their children into danger of pregnancy outside marriage, or at the best, into early marriages that prevent a mature understanding of one's proper partner and that invite early divorce.

For the parents' clubs looking for ammunition against the local social climbers' insistence on grammar school proms, mixed swimming parties, and paired-off dances, this book is also a "must." It shows what happens to teen-agers who are thrust into each other's company before they are psychologically aware of their own selves to value the permanent and solid constraint necessary to form a successful family life.

Dr. Duvall's well-known opinions against premature dating do not appear too explicitly in these pages, since the age-level often seems that of college life. But the conclusions remain the same, no matter who reads these pages — the junior high, senior high, or college student, or the parent who wants to have a proper family atmosphere.

The only danger in giving Dr. Duvall's book the praise which it deserves is that the reader would discard the judgment as too favorable to be true. But favorable it must be, and to a superlative degree. There is not a single line in it that is inapplicable to a Catholic approach to sexual morality. This does not mean that the book is a Catholic moral treatise. The author does not base her conclusions on Catholic moral theology but rather on statistical, psychological, and sociological considerations. These conclusions are, however, quite in accord with sound Catholic moral teaching.

FRANCIS L. FILAS, S.J.
Chairman, Department of Theology
Loyola University, Chicago

Contents

1 *What Are Your*

Y ou may feel unsure about the sexual side of life. Most people are confused about their standards of behavior. It is hard to know with certainty what is right and what is wrong today. Few responsible persons can tell you definitely what is expected and what is forbidden, and why.

You may know a great deal about the birds, bees, and babies. But when it comes to knowing how far to go on a date, that is something else again. Developing your own standards is not easy. Expressing your feelings and even knowing for sure what it is that you are feeling for any given person at a particular moment are complicated considerations.

You do not want to get in too deep, but you do not relish being aloof or left out, either. You do not want to be labeled an "ice cube" or be considered too prudish to express affection. You want to be loved and to love in all the special ways that are so important now while you are young, as well as through the lifetime that lies ahead.

You have already discovered that the sexual aspect of life is full of contradictions in our modern world. Before you were old enough to know what it was all about, you sensed that sex is something that many people do not discuss freely. Candid, comfortable discussion of sex is avoided in many a school and church. Sex is not openly talked about in some families. Yet sex appeal is used as a lure throughout the business and entertainment worlds, to the point where some observers say that we live in a sex-saturated society.

You have been told that we Americans believe in premarital chastity, and that a boy and girl should save sex for marriage. But teen-agers in our country have great freedom today, and freedom opens the possibility of becoming too involved. Harsh penalties ensue when two of you get into trouble. Most families are a long way from condoning behavior that oversteps their bounds. In many a modern community the young person of either sex who behaves irresponsibly finds doors closed to him. Former friends are busy. Future education is endangered. Members of the family act as though they have been disgraced. Mothers cry, fathers rant, and all the furies of social ostracism descend upon the wayward ones.

You recall still other contradictions about sex in your world today. With such widely different and completely opposite forces

Sex Standards?

at work, is it any wonder that so many are uncertain about what is right? A young person is bound to be confused today.

Sex Standards in America

Consider the range of attitudes toward sex conduct in almost any modern community. Every stance from the most conventional to the most completely permissive is expressed. Here are five commonly found in America today:

1. Chastity before marriage
"Abstinence before marriage is an absolute requisite"
"Something should be held sacred until marriage"
"Obligations go with rights; therefore sex belongs in marriage alone"

2. Chastity of women, but not of men
"The double standard is not fair, but it makes sense as long as it is women who have the babies"
"Abstinence before marriage is not so necessary for the boy"
"As a man, I set my own standards, but when I marry, it will be to a virgin"

3. Sexual freedom between lovers
"When two people really love one another, what they do is their own business"
"A couple's love is their own to express as they see fit"
"When you are in love, marriage is just a technicality"

4. Sexual permissiveness
"Whatever you can get away with is permissible"
"A fellow is entitled to anything that a girl allows"
"Anything goes as long as it's fun"

5. Sexual irresponsibility
"Who am I to say what is right and what is wrong?"
"Brighter minds than mine have come to no conclusion about sex"
"Do whatever you feel like at the moment—that's my motto"

No doubt you already have heard statements like these from persons your own age or older. You sense that it makes a difference whether sex partners are strangers, casual acquaintances, familiar friends, sweethearts, or lovers about to be married. Still another factor in the complex equation is the relative mutuality or exploitativeness of the relationship.

Moral Questions Stir College Campuses

With answers so hard to come by, you naturally look to the way students on college campuses solve their problems of sex conduct before marriage. Whether or not you are university-minded, you are interested in what students on various campuses say. Yet here, too, you meet with a wide variety of opinions and conduct.

The president of Vassar College opened a Pandora's box when she told her students that the behavior expected of them did not include premarital sex relations. Some 40 per cent of the 1,450 students spoke up promptly, saying that what they did in their private lives was their own business. Yet more than one-half of the girls upheld the president's position, saying for instance,

> This college would not be respected if it did not take a stand for the dignity of young women. Drunkenness and premarital relations do not dignify personal freedom for me.
> We are not yet adults and the college should be able to exert a certain amount of control over our social behavior.
> (Quoted from *The New York Times,* May 9, 1962)

Minor skirmishes of the same sort on other campuses were overshadowed by the storm at Harvard over allowing girls to visit men in their rooms. Dr. Graham B. Blaine, Jr., psychiatrist to the Harvard and Radcliffe Health Service, said in *The New York Times* of January 16, 1964:

> Universities that allow unrestricted use of bedrooms by men and women even for a few hours each week cannot help but be understood by students to be condoning or encouraging sexual intercourse. ... While greater liberality in regard to sexual behavior is evident throughout the country, the average American family does not allow its son or daughter to entertain the opposite sex in a bedroom.

These incidents are representative of the confusion about sexual behavior that is found on most college campuses today. The young man who has not clarified his own sex standards by the time he gets to college, finds himself hard-pressed to know where to turn when he arrives on campus. It is even more difficult for a girl, because she is urged to "express herself," not only by some of the college men she dates, but also by some upper-class women students.

There are students who are taking a firm stand. An open letter in a campus paper reads in part:

> We are in revolt against the line of the "new morality" that is forced down our throats by books, magazines, television, films, professors and some churchmen. Sex, violence, lust and godlessness are taking over the nation. When venereal disease among young Americans rises 130% between 1956 and 1961, when 13,000,000 children come from broken homes—who is responsible? *We are.*

Newspapers and magazines go into elaborate detail about the wild escapades and extremist thinking of *some* students on *some* campuses, leaving the impression that *all* students today are involved in a great deal of sexual activity. Yet the studies of campus morals and the experience of some of us in the position to know tell quite a different story. Your author, who meets personally with young people from more than one hundred campuses across the country in a given year, knows how distressingly distorted most of these news stories are. We do not question that the cases reported actually happened. We do most vigorously assert that they give a biased view of youth today.

If you have ever resented the way stories about juvenile delinquents outnumber the accounts of teen-agers in wholesome pursuits, you know how such news stories distort reality. So it is on many a college campus. The great majority of students are responsible young people working hard to get their degrees and make something of themselves. Their fun is well within bounds most of the time. When a few of them do get out of line, their escapades receive a lot of publicity because they are unusual rather than typical.

Keep in mind, too, what Dr. Celia Deschin said in connection with her study of teen-agers:

> It is one of the paradoxes of the 20th century culture in the U. S. that while interest in and preoccupation with sex have greatly increased, knowledge about sex—its meaning and relation to wholesome family life—has not increased appreciably. On the contrary there are indications of chaos and confusion despite the plethora of books, pamphlets and magazines, as well as reports of studies of sex behavior, most of which deal with college students.

Adults Do Not Agree

Grown-ups do not agree on how far to go before marriage. Some adults, remembering the damage done by old-fashioned prudery, go to the other extreme. They advocate sexual permissiveness without full recognition of the effect it has upon individuals or their families now and in the years ahead.

The chances are that your religious leaders and most of your teachers hold much more conventional points of view. They usually advocate premarital chastity and marital fidelity. But these more conservative adults are often unable to tell you *why* they take the stands they do. Sometimes they hedge and avoid the issue rather than be considered old-fashioned by the young moderns around them. As Dr. Blaine, the Harvard psychiatrist quoted above, says:

> Moral injunctions against premarital sexual activity are less clearly spoken in today's world. Many of the religious leaders who deal directly with college students are reluctant to make an emotional or spiritual appeal for adherence to the old standards for fear of being ridiculed by the more science-oriented, materialistic students who take nothing on faith but instead demand a logical reason for every rule. Actually, these students are a vocal minority that does not deserve the attention given it by those who should be more concerned with the substantial portion of the student population that is looking to religion for support for its own high standards.

Church leaders in many denominations are concerned about premarital sex relations of their young people but have done little about it. Counselors in schools and deans in colleges have been deliberating the question of what they can do to guide their students, but to date little consensus has been reached.

Teachers and administrators have tried to introduce the kinds of courses that would be personally helpful to students in school. Some have demonstrated how helpful such programs can be. Other courses have had to be discontinued, sometimes because of lack of good teachers, sometimes because of disagreement or confusion in the community about what could and should be done in the classroom.

Parents, too, are confused. Some think that young people know a great deal more than you do about life and love and sex, and what to do about it. When they say anything at all, it is apt to be too "preachy" or heavy-handed to help. Some teen-agers see adults as so judgmental that they keep things from their parents for fear of punishment. This conspiracy of silence leaves parents often in the dark, anxious and afraid.

Studies show that young people generally are reluctant to discuss with parents their questions of love, sex, petting, engagement, and marriage. These are the questions that are most urgent in a young person's life, and you want straight answers to them. Most of the time you talk over these issues with other young people. They will be honest with you, usually, but most of them are no more sure of themselves than you are. Sometimes you wish that responsible adults would come out and say what they really mean, instead of hedging the issues.

You are so used to double-talk that straightforward convictions may startle you. You may hear so many warnings about not being "square" that you may pull up short when you read how one businessman pleaded for "the return of the square" not long ago:

> We would be for participation and against sitting life out.
> . . . simplicity and against sophistication . . . for laughter and against sniggering . . . for America and against her enemies . . . for the direct and against the devious . . . for the honest way against the easy short cut . . . for a well-done job and against the goof-off . . . for education and against the pretense of learning . . . for building and against tearing down . . . for the boys and girls who excel and against the international bedroom athletes . . .

One girl who as yet had not been swayed by the arguments she heard for sex thrills before marriage told her father that sometimes she wondered what she was waiting for. He wisely replied, "I think I can tell you in six words what you are waiting for. You are waiting to be free. Free from the nagging voice of conscience and the gray shadow of guilt. Free to give all of yourself, not a panicky fraction. Tell your open-minded friends not to be so open-minded that their brains fall out." This is the lesson to be learned from the common pin that has a head to keep it from going too far.

One definition of progress describes education as man's going forward from cocksure ignorance to thoughtful uncertainty. This is the climate of opinion in your world today, and the big reason why even adults do not agree upon sex standards.

The Problem Used to Be Simpler

How far to go in expressing your feelings is no idle academic question for you. Almost any evening—either with familiar friend or fresh first date—the whole matter can open up in ways that cannot be side-stepped. You *have* to know what your standards are, and why. You are often alone with your date. The evening is full of stimulation. The music throbs around you with its tantalizing beat. Your mind is filled with thoughts more exciting than even the wide screen you watch together. You want to hold and to be held. You long to be close to one another. You have more to say than words, more to express than kisses. So, what do you do?

This situation would not have arisen at the turn of the century. Then a good girl was carefully guarded by her family. She entertained her fellow on the front porch or in the back parlor within earshot of her parents. Mother or Dad might come in unannounced with a bowl of apples or a pitcher of lemonade at any moment—a fact fully realized by the visiting swain and his girl.

Of course, there were men and boys who visited women "of easy virtue" in town. But when they did, they had no question about what it was they were after. The women lived in red-light districts, where they made a business of attending to men's sexual desires. The young fellow could, if he wished, resort to sowing his wild oats—this was allowed under the double standard that was tacitly condoned.

Even the wildest young fellow expected to marry "a good girl" eventually. Virginity was much to be desired in unmarried women, and brides were expected to merit the white wedding gown that denotes purity. The traditional code called for premarital chastity and postmarital fidelity, at least for the girl, who was after all to be the mother of a man's children. Many men felt strongly that a man, as well as the girl he married, should postpone sexual experience until marriage. The church left no doubt of its position. Its voicing of "right" and "wrong" was loud and clear.

Two great world wars, millions of families moving from place to place, increased prosperity, lots of automobiles, and plenty of leisure time have changed a great deal of life around us. Boys who went off to military service heard the other fellows brag of their conquests. Girls and boys went to large co-educational schools and then on to colleges and universities where they had contact with others whose standards were different from those in which they had been brought up. "Nice kids" in time discovered what the not-so-nice ones were up to, as each learned from the others.

Now shady stories and questionable pictures are swapped by grade-school boys. Girls are under constant pressure to measure up to the most seductive dimensions. Magazines and movies openly portray in exaggerated detail forms of sexuality that used to be left to the imagination. The climate of opinion has shifted from restraint to indulgence. Once a mother bade her daughter good-by as she left for the evening with her boy friend with the caution, "Be careful, dear." Now the parting good-by from many a mother and father is, "Have fun."

You have grown up wanting to have fun. Your generation has had more money and more ways to spend it on pleasure than any previous generation anywhere. You have parents who grew up in the Great Depression and vowed that you children would have everything they were denied when they were young. You have been pushed, often before you were ready, into boy-girl parties and a sophisticated social life.

Young people your age go on single dates with each other. They go steady, or steadily, from the beginning of their aquaintance. They are thrown together constantly in the social life of your school. They see a great deal of one another, and are seen by you who know them as "belonging to each other."

Going on car dates offers almost unlimited freedom. The boy picks up his date at her home, and within a few minutes they are off on their own. Where they go, and what they do, is up to them. Every community has its "lovers' lane" where parked cars provide almost any degree of intimate interaction. Drive-in theaters are called "passion pits" in recognition of the activities that go on quite apart from the movie that is being shown. Double dates are no safeguard these days, especially when the other couple brings liquor along. It is no wonder that those who "get caught" so often cite the automobile as the scene of their involvement.

The girl's or boy's home is convenient for their love-making in many a case. Mother and Father often are gone for predictable intervals through the day and evening. Nowadays it is unlikely that a resident aunt or grandmother or other relative keeps an eye on things at home, as once might have been the case. So, what a teen-ager does while at home with some special guest is up to them alone.

All this new freedom brings with it a great deal of responsibility. All around you, you see evidence of what happens when young people do not assume full responsibility for their conduct. Some of your classmates already have cracked up in some sex jam or "have-to" marriage that makes you realize what a hazard irresponsibility is. Others of your acquaintance avoid the whole issue by having little to do with members of the other sex. Some of your more thoughtful friends make a point of staying away from those social functions that might lead to trouble. You may find both of these extremes unacceptable personally. You want to date and have friends of both sexes. You want to be popular and go to the social events that your school and community offer. Yet you may not be quite sure of yourself or of how you should handle any of the complicated situations that almost surely will be involved when you do participate.

No wonder you want to clarify your own feelings and attitudes, standards, and values. You do not want to be pressured into something that does not make sense to you. You want real reasons for what you do. You need some solid basis for saying "No" to the conduct that does not fit into your way of life. You want some sense of direction that allows you to say "Yes" to all the fun and fulfillment that could be yours.

You realize that your life is a part of today's world and that what you do matters. The President of the Carnegie Corporation writes:

> Each generation refights the crucial battles and either brings new vitality to the ideals or allows them to decay . . . the moral order is not something enshrined in historic documents, or stowed away like the family silver. It is a living, changing thing, and never any better than the generation that holds it in trust. A society is continuously re-created, for good or ill, by its members. This will strike some as burdensome, but it will summon others to greatness.

2 Everyone Does It
— Or Do They?

One of the loudest arguments for going all the way before marriage is that everyone else is doing it. This simply is not true. Ever since 1915 there have been dozens of studies of premarital sex behavior, not one of which suggests even remotely that virginity is no more.

The well-known Kinsey reports are widely misquoted as finding that premarital sex experience is practically universal. Actually, Dr. Kinsey and his staff found nothing of the sort. Among sixteen- to twenty-year-old college-bound boys, more than half (58 per cent) were without sex experience. Fully 80 per cent of the twenty-year-old unmarried women were virgins.

The Kinsey reports were published more than ten years ago, but more recent studies of members of both sexes fail to turn up more startling incidences of premarital intimacy. Professor Ehrmann's intensive research found 87 per cent of the women and 43 per cent of the nonveteran men college students were without sex experience. The best educated guess is that perhaps half the men and one-fourth of the women college students have had coital experience by the time they reach twenty-one.

Those who are counted as nonvirgins include all who at any time, with anyone, have gone all the way. The boy who engaged in some youthful indiscretion is included as well as the "wolf" who prowls every week. The couple who love one another and plan on marriage is included along with those more casual in their contact. Yet *most* college-bound students are found to be virgins. This is remarkable.

Possibly in no other area do so many refrain from any single instance of overstepping bounds. Which of you could honestly report that you have never taken anything that did not belong to you? that you have never lied? that you have never cheated? that you have never broken a law? Yet, among those of you destined for college, the majority never yet has participated in sexual intercourse.

It is true that young people who drop out of school, or fail to finish high school, are more likely to be unhappy about themselves, and to be more sexually experienced than are those who graduate and go on to college. But even among those of you who are not college-bound, sex experience cannot be assumed.

Among some young rebels, there is a show of sophistication that far exceeds their actual experience. One account in *Time* magazine tells of a group of teen-age boys doing poorly in school, and heading into trouble, who insisted on being seen together. They showed up in flashy clothes, laughed too loudly, and chain-smoked with intensity. They poked fun at the adult leader for wearing "square" clothes and not appearing "hep." They discussed sex with bravado but were found to be utterly ignorant of the subject, and in spite of all their talk, they all were virgins (a fact they would have denied loudly, no doubt).

Listen to those who argue loudest for sexual permissiveness, and you sense their own uncertainty. The person who is sure of his ground does not have to pressure others into following his lead. It is the individual who has some serious doubts about himself that boasts the most.

Premarital intercourse presents a dilemma. Professors Burgess and Wallin found three ways in which the couples they studied from engagement into marriage dealt with the sex-before-marriage problem. First were the couples both of whose members were firmly opposed to going all the way until they had married. Their ideals made them relatively free from strain and conflict. Second were the couples who agreed that intercourse was all right for them. They were sure of their love. They were unconcerned about pregnancy, and they had no doubts. So their behavior seemed to constitute no problem for them. The majority of the engaged couples were in conflict about their behavior. If they did go all the way, they were often disillusioned, distressed, and disturbed. When they stopped short of coitus, they were physically unsatisfied. The investigators conclude, "Many couples find themselves sorely tried in refraining from intercourse, but by no means entirely happy or conscience-free if they yield."

There are all kinds of people, in sex behavior as in everything else. Some are openly promiscuous, many are faithful to their one and only. Some flout the conventional standards, others uphold them. Some engage in premarital sex play and brag about it, others are ashamed of it. Some are quietly intimate, others just as quietly are chaste.

Studies of premarital sex behavior suggest the kinds of persons who go all the way before marriage, and the kinds who tend more often to follow the code of chastity. Reviewing some of these distinctions between those who do and those who do not wait until marriage may serve as a guide to what to expect of yourself and others, generally.

Who Upholds High Standards?

Girls, more than boys, enter marriage as virgins. Male sexual feelings are more urgent than are the female's, especially among unmarried young people. The teen-age boy is aware of being sexually stimulated in ways that few girls recognize. The boy is more sex-driven than is the girl. Throughout life the fellow is more easily aroused by more stimuli than are girls and women.

It is not only that the two sexes differ biologically. They are brought up to feel differently about themselves. Boys are taught to be men—to be strong, forceful, active, and capable of functioning in manly ways. Being sexually virile means a great deal to a young man. It can be even more important to the teen-age boy who is beginning to find himself. He needs to prove to himself and others that he is capable of functioning like a man, either in direct sex expression, or in responsibility for sexual restraint.

Girls generally are not sexually awakened until after they have begun regular sex experience, usually after their marriage. They are brought up to value the emotional and social aspects of life between the sexes, and to be more cautious about direct sex expression. After all, if something goes wrong, it is the girl who has the baby.

Middle-class young people are taught to wait. The sons and daughters of "nice families" usually have dreams and aspirations that would be incompatible with early sexual activity. They are aware of its risks, and choose to wait till marriage, in many cases. Those who go on through school and prepare for good positions tend to postpone sexual intimacy until they are ready to settle down and have a family.

Fellows and girls who feel they have little to look forward to in life often get a "what's the use" attitude. They feel that no one cares what they do, or what happens to them. Not infrequently they come from homes in which adults have been disheartened from the time they, too, were young. They grow up in families where sex is taken for granted as an acceptable immediate satisfaction. Some of them and eventually their babies are brought up with government support and financial assistance from private and public agencies—from one generation to the next. This conflicts with the American belief that no one need remain a prisoner of the class of his birth.

The privileged boy from the better part of town may take advantage of a "lower-class" girl. He is more apt to seek out such a girl for sheer sex without caring for her as a person than he would a girl from a background like his own. He may be ostracized by the "nice" girls because of his reputation for being wild. He may get caught and have to marry a girl whose pregnancy he allegedly has caused. If he is a good catch, the girl may "put out" in order to snare him into marriage. This appears to be one reason why many boys marry "down" at the same time that girls tend to marry fellows either from their own cultural level or a step or two above.

Dr. Ehrmann, who has studied these relationships intensively, says that boys tend to descend the social ladder in order to find willing sexual partners. For the lower-status girl, association with such a fellow may be a gamble, but she risks it because she has her main chance—marriage—in mind.

Education Is Related to Chastity

Numerous studies show that the more education a young person has or aspires to, the less tendency there is to go all the way before marriage. Boys and girls who graduate from school and go on for further advanced training are more apt to wait until they marry before starting full intimacy than are those who drop out of school with slight or no expectation of further education.

There are several reasons why education makes such a difference. The boy or girl whose dream of the future includes becoming prepared for a career in business or in one of the professions has too much at stake to take a chance on losing it all in irresponsible sexual activity.

Generally speaking, those who go on for advanced education tend to be the more responsible persons. They have to exercise discipline in order to study and to become competent in the fields of their choice. They tend to care what happens to both their friends and themselves. They sense their worth as persons enough to be protective and disciplined in interaction.

In contrast, the young person who drops out of school before he or she has developed his talents and abilities fully tends to have a lower estimation of his own worth. He is more likely to have the attitude that puts having fun ahead of postponing immediate satisfaction for future fulfillment. Putting present pleasure ahead of long-range goals is characteristic of children, indicating lack of maturity, generally.

The better-educated sections of the population live in neighborhoods where responsible behavior is expected. Anarchy in sex or anything else makes less sense to those who have a big investment in life. So you find that fathers, mothers, neighbors, teachers, and friends of one's own age expect a degree of personal and social responsibility of the youth in the area. Although at times the behavior of young people and adults gets out of line, the norm is chastity before marriage and fidelity thereafter.

There is a relationship between stable family life and education. Those who drop out of school or settle for less education than is available to them tend to marry early, to have more difficulty in their marriages, and more often break up in divorce, separation, or annulment than do those who get a good education before they marry. Another way of looking at this is to recognize that those who value marriage and family life tend also to feel that education is well worth the time and money it costs. Those who act on impulse with little thought for the future are more often among those who do not wait for marriage before becoming sexually active.

These general statements aren't intended as criticism of persons who are unable to set long-term goals for themselves because they are limited by social or economic disadvantages. Young people who have these handicaps merit special understanding and encouragement.

Needing Love Makes a Difference

The young person who feels unloved, misunderstood, rejected, and neglected is far more likely to indulge in premarital sexual intercourse than is the one who knows real and continuing love. Sex is so easily confused with love that it takes an emotionally secure young person to appraise his or her feelings.

A girl may yield to the love-talk of a boy for whom she really cares little, or may not even know, just for the sake of a little loving in her life. She mistakes the boy's desire for the loving care for which she hungers. She yields to his intimate fondling to prove to herself that she is lovable. The tragedy is that the boy who takes advantage of such a girl usually does not love her, or even respect her as a person. Because she is obviously available, he takes her, much as he would take any freely offered morsel. He tires of her in time, and she has nowhere to go but into the arms of some other exploitative male, who uses her for what he selfishly wants with little concern for her. Since she values herself so cheaply, she finds few boys or men who cherish her, and rarely finds the love for which she longs.

Love-hungry boys are vulnerable too. They tend to go further in their sex play than does the fellow who knows that his family loves and cares for him. The boy who has the feeling no one cares what he does tries in every way he can to feel wanted and loved. He deceives himself that loving up a girl is the same as loving her, or being loved by her. He goes too quickly to the biological response in his urgency to get an emotionally satisfying experience. It is only after he has gone the limit that he discovers that it leaves him feeling empty, unfulfilled, and unsatisfied in everything but the physical release itself.

A recent study of more than one thousand college students found fewer men having premarital sexual intercourse with girls they loved than with girl friends or acquaintances. When a fellow loves a girl, he cherishes her and wants to have things just right. So he is more likely to forego sexual relations with the girl he loves and wants to marry than he would be with a pick-up, a casual date, or a girl he does not care about.

Being in love makes a girl somewhat more willing to go all the way with her sweetheart. The evidence is that women's sexual expression is primarily and profoundly related to being in love. It is when a female is in love that she is least on guard and most erotically stimulated. Professor Ehrmann's conclusion is that "being in love means a decrease among males and an increase among females in the incidence of premarital sexual intercourse and in the personal acceptance of such behavior."

One other big difference in love between the sexes is that girls tend to become emotionally attached to their sex partners more than their partners are to them. This leads to the familiar heartbreak of a girl who has given herself to the man she thinks she loves, and then finds that he tires of her and breaks off the relationship at the point when she becomes too demanding. It is just when she most wants to marry her lover that he is most apt to feel trapped and tied down. A good many couples break up because they have become too sexually involved before marriage.

"Everyone Does It" Only in Certain Sets

Any high school, college, or community is made up of a variety of social sets. Each of these subcultures has its own standards and expectations of its members. There are some sexy cliques in which going all the way is condoned, even expected. There are many other groupings in which young people of both sexes enjoy each other as persons. They meet around such interests as sports, music, dramatics, hobbies, outdoor activities, science clubs, and service organizations with little direct sexual expression of their interest in one another until they are ready to choose their mates and proceed into marriage.

Going along with a crowd whose standards differ from yours is self-defeating. Conforming to what they expect only brings you shame, guilt, and self-recrimination. Identifying with those who are not basically your kind of people is no kindness to them or to you in the long run.

It need not be too painful to give up associates with whom you do not feel you belong. Actually, your friends may not have been purposely chosen in the first place. Oftentimes they "happen" by accident of proximity or interest. The chances are that you got in with them originally through some shared activity. As your interests and pursuits shift, your friends do too, naturally. One of the ways to break off an unsatisfactory friendship is to develop new interests and activities.

Moving to a new community is another way you change your group loyalties. As you establish yourself in the new location, you find the persons who are doing the things you enjoy and upholding the standards that you can accept. Even if you do not actually move to another community, you can shift your associations to another quarter. After a while you find the friends, the interests, and pursuits that are most meaningful to you.

Such decisions are not simple. They are made after a great deal of fumbling around and thinking through what kind of person you are and what you really want most out of life. When you get to the point where you are fed up with pressures to conform to standards that do not make sense to you, you still have a choice. No one is forcing you to do what you do not want to, 'way down deep within you. Whenever you want to badly enough, you can stop unsatisfactory behavior and begin to behave in ways that are more personally fulfilling.

Most Americans Believe Waiting till Marriage Is Best

There have been many studies of how Americans feel about sex standards and behavior. One television poll on "Sex and Morals" in June, 1964, analyzed responses to a number of pertinent questions from fifteen thousand individuals of all ages. Three-fourths of the men and four-fifths of the women felt that moral standards are declining as evidenced by such phenomena as "anything goes, too much interest in sex, family instability, premarital sex, and promiscuity."

The majority of both adults (68 per cent) and teen-agers (60 per cent) felt that sex standards are freer now than they used to be and "that's bad." All ages concurred that parents are not strict enough today in supervising their children. When asked if premarital sexual relations are all right for engaged couples, only 4 per cent said "Yes." A clear majority of 56 per cent thought premarital experience among engaged couples was definitely wrong and immoral; another 19 per cent considered it questionable; and 14 per cent said, "It depends." Sex before and outside of marriage is clearly frowned upon.

At the 1961 Conference of the National Council on Family Relations, Dr. Amy Gerling reported on a study of midwestern college students and their parents. Fathers, mothers, sons, and daughters all were opposed to engaged couples having sexual relations. When they reacted to the statement, "Premarital sex relations are all right for people who are engaged and going to be married," 93 per cent of the mothers and 84 per cent of the college girls disagreed with it. Some 83 per cent of the fathers and a clear majority of the sons (52 per cent) disagreed with the suggestion that it is all right for engaged couples to have sexual intercourse. Dr. Gerling summarizes her findings in this way: "both parents and students appear to be more 'moral,' that is more frequently 'on the side of the angels' than current discussions of the state of our society's morals would lead one to expect."

Your author's study of university freshman girls, reported in February, 1964, found 88 per cent disagreeing with the dating-scale statement, "It is not important for a person to remain pure until marriage." A full 92 per cent disagreed with the suggestion, "Young people should make as much love on a date as they wish"; and 94 per cent disagreed with the statement, "When two people are serious about each other, it is all right for them to make any kind of love." Moreover, "student scores became more conservative as dating involvement increased, declining steadily from those going steady to those being engaged to the most conservative accrued by those who were already married."

Review of sex standards among today's young Americans leads to the conclusion that most men as well as women feel that abstinence before marriage is really best. A majority of even those men who accept the double standard that gives men sexual freedom denied girls before marriage, say that chastity is the best policy for both sexes. Professor Reiss concludes his study of premarital sexual standards in America with the observation that traditional teachings still hold. Abstinence still has a strong grip on a great number of today's young people, who feel that they love each other too much to risk spoiling their relationship with premature sex experience. As one young man told Professor Burgess,

> We have discussed sexual relations and we both decided we'd rather not. It's not because we don't want to, but because we don't think it is worth it. And it's not because of any risk involved. I thought I would cheapen myself in my eyes and hers. I love her too much to have that relationship a furtive one.

The conclusion is that everyone does not go in for premarital sexual activity. Some young people talk big about their sexual exploits. There are those who do go all the way in practice. But in any school, college, or community there are enough of those who prefer to wait until marriage, so that a fellow or girl who wants to be one of them has plenty of company. The weight of the evidence is still on the side of chastity.

3 It's Natural

$\int$ ex is universal among mammals. Boys and girls, men and women share with many other forms of nature the ability to reproduce by the mating of male and female to bring forth young of the species. In this respect, sex is natural.

But the argument that because sexual intercourse is natural, it is all right between a boy and girl before marriage, fails to take into consideration a number of important factors. These can be spelled out by any thinking young person who cares to look at the nature of human nature.

The Nature of Human Nature

One of the first things to realize is that human beings, being mammals, share many common physical characteristics with cats, dogs, lions, and porpoises. But that is not to say that just because we all are mammalian, we therefore should act like animals.

A cat teases her prey and plays with the mouse or the bird she has caught before she eventually eats it. Although there are some humans who are almost that cruel with those they take advantage of, we do not approve of such behavior. A woman who even speaks hostilely of another is called "catty," which is anything but a pleasant appellation.

A male tomcat takes any female who will receive him, and wanders off to others with no further thought or care for any of the females he has taken. Each mother cat has her kittens and raises them herself without any help from their father. This is acceptable in the feline world, but is loudly condemned among humans.

Judge Jennie Loitman Barron, on the bench for twenty-five years, expresses widespread indignation when she tells of the appalling number of superior girls she sees in trouble. They are not the tough skid-row girls she used to see in court, but fine young women from good homes who have been admitted to the best colleges. Yet they end up in despair because they have been trapped by their own misinterpretation of the nature of human sex experience.

Says Judge Barron:

I am thinking of one particular girl who came to me. When she was seventeen, she stepped from a warm life at home into the sophisticated college world. Without preparation, she was thrown into the company of older girls from broken or permissive homes where no limits were set on behavior, some defiant girls rebelling against authority, and some girls whose parents were spiritually bankrupt.

The girl who came to me for help had brought from home moral standards that many of her pseudo-sophisticated dormmates found amusing. They told her she would have a dull time unless she quit being so old-fashioned.

In her sophomore year, after six weeks of steady dating, she was "pinned" by a sophisticated young man, a senior. He began to demand privileges, arguing about "the rightness" of intimacy between two people in love. The girl discussed his arguments with her dorm-mates, many of whom were already sleeping with their dates. Their advice was to forget scruples.

Exposed to this atmosphere, suggesting that sex was exciting, desirable, even healthy, she submitted to her young man. As she became more deeply involved, she began to tell herself that what she was doing was right. She always got back to her dormitory before curfew, but on week ends she could leave campus, ostensibly to go home to visit relatives. School officials never checked up on her whereabouts.

Her affair was conducted in a nearby woods, in the boy's room and in motels. There was no hint of trouble until she received an unexpected letter from the boy, telling her he was returning home to marry a girl he had known since childhood. She was stunned with disbelief. A short time later she discovered she was pregnant.

It was at this point she arrived in my private chambers appealing for help. I tried to persuade her to confide in her parents, so that they could help her in this frightening experience. She refused. Then she had an abortion performed in another state over a week end.

Returning to her studies, she could no longer concentrate. Her grades began to fall. She was warned by the dean's office that the college would have to notify her parents. Her world crumbled about her, and at the end of the semester she dropped out of college.

This girl was the victim not only of male indifference, as the judge suggests, but also of her own mistaken view of sex. She did not see that sex "naturally" includes the whole process of courtship, marriage, coitus, pregnancy, childbirth, and child-rearing in families—in that order.

In behaving like a healthy young animal, she endangered her relationship with her sweetheart, and eventually lost him. She gambled with her education as a woman, and lost out at college. She risked the life of her baby and lost that, too. She lost, for the time, a sense of who she was as a person, and so threw away months, maybe years of her life.

The simple fact is—you are not an animal, and cannot safely act like one without sacrificing much that is important in your life as a human being. One of the most widely discussed novels of recent years is William Golding's *Lord of the Flies*. The power of the book, and the movie made from it, lies in its portrayal of what happens when human beings, even young boys, revert to bestiality. Man may be biologically an animal, but is not a beast.

Like Golding, writers such as J. D. Salinger and Tennessee Williams have captured the imagination of your generation. Their appeal is essentially that of realism. You do not like phoniness. You want a world in which people are honest with you and with themselves. You prefer straight talk to flowery circumlocution. You abhor hypocrisy in which men preach one thing and practice another. All this is good.

But sometimes the fault in this realism is that it leaves the impression that all life is cheap and shabby. It focuses so clearly on the disreputable that the beauty of the human spirit is ignored. Sweetness and light leave a sticky taste in the mouth. But a steady diet of sin and lust can make you sick. Man is not angelic; neither is he all bad. Most men, like you and me, are aspiring sinners. They know they fall short of their highest possibilities, yet they continue to try to realize their full potential. They take their daily frustrations because their dreams and ideals give them courage to continue. And, what's wrong with that?

Man Is More Than an Animal

One of the profound facts about human nature is that man is more, much more than a physical body. Mankind around the world eats to satisfy his hunger for food, a process which he shares with the animal world. But there the similarity ends. Food has significance for man beyond just the eating itself. Family members eat together as one way of expressing their unity and togetherness. In the business world, contracts are sealed over a cup of coffee, and plans are laid over a shared meal. When human beings want to entertain one another, or to be gracious and friendly, they bring on food to eat together—a pattern that is found around the world.

You enjoy eating in the ways that are socially, aesthetically, and emotionally satisfying. Just because you follow the forms that are expected does not mean that you do not taste the food and savor it fully. In fact, the more ceremony there is, the more you like it, as in the cutting of your birthday or wedding cake, for instance.

That man does not live by bread alone is a well-known piece of wisdom. Man is more than flesh and blood: he is mind and spirit. He has feelings, preferences, and ways of doing things that are important for his fulfillment, or even for his enjoyment.

Sex is truly satisfying when it is within the settings and circumstances that you have learned to think of as right for you. Through the centuries that men and women have lived together, certain ways have emerged that make sense for the man, the woman, their children, and their world.

The predatory male may move from female to female but he misses out on the lasting satisfactions of family life. He has little of the tenderness and care that permanent faithfulness to a loving wife provides. He has none of the comfort of a lifelong companion upon whom he can count, no matter what. He does not get the chance to feel a part of the flow of the generations as the father of a family does. He may not even know his children, whose growing up he has little, if any, part of. He grows old alone and lonely without the security that being a faithful family man might have brought him.

The woman has even more to lose when she sees sex as natural for herself as a female animal. She loses the possibility of the devotion and care of a good man throughout her life. She loses the likelihood of a home of her own. She loses her reputation, her standing, her status among respectable women everywhere. She loses the feeling of being personally worthy. In time, as she ages, she loses even her temporary male companions, as they turn to younger sex partners.

The children of men and women who take their sex where they find it—what of them? Who could really enjoy being illegitimate, not knowing for sure who his father was? How does a young person feel whose parents are not faithful to one another? How important is it that a youngster have a secure family life with parents who love one another through the years?

But wait, you say. "Sure I'll settle down when the time comes, but right now it's only natural that I get some release." You may just do that. But, remember that the overwhelming tendency is to continue doing what you have done before.

The chances are that you speak much as you have been doing

through the years. You can tell a man from New England from a fellow from the deep South, as soon as you hear him talk. Why? Because each man tends to speak as he learned to talk when he was growing up. Is there any reason to believe that the same thing does not happen in sexual expression? If a fellow always has played fast and loose with girls, is he sure to drop all these habits once he gets married? Will he no longer be attracted to other women? If he is, will he not want to do as he always has before, and make a play for them? What assurance have you that the marriage ceremony will change the kind of thing you always have done?

How Can You Be Sure?

The only thing you can be fairly sure about is that you will probably be very much the same person after you marry that you have been before. Getting married is a big step, but it cannot change human nature. You need not kid yourself that when you marry, either you or your mate will all of a sudden be something neither of you has been before. You cannot hope to reform your partner or yourself. You both may become more mature. You may settle down, at least for a while. But you will always be the kind of personalities you brought to your marriage in the first place.

The only way you can be sure of your partner is to expect him realistically to continue to be himself. This is well known. It is probably the reason why even the most sophisticated young man prefers to marry "a good girl" who has not played around before she marries. Professor Ehrmann found less than one-half (47 per cent) of the men he studied willing to marry a nonvirgin; and the Kinsey reports of almost three thousand men found but 53 per cent willing to marry girls who were not virgins.

This by no means suggests that there is no hope for the girl Judge Barron was concerned about. If she learns from her experience, she may recover from her hurt and mature into a fine woman, wife, and mother. The big factor will be her attitude toward herself and men. When she finds it possible to recognize that she made a dreadful mistake and is able to pick herself up and go on, confident that she will never be quite so foolhardy again, the chances for her future are good.

One big hazard today is rationalizing what one has done as right and "natural." The unfortunate girl's dorm-mates fell into this trap. Because some of them were going all the way with their dates, they talked loud and persuasively about how natural and normal it was.

It is the person who brags about the foolish episodes in his life that finds it hardest to face them for what they are. He runs the risk of convincing himself as well as others that his strength lies in his weakest moments. Not recognizing the error of his ways, he cannot forgive himself nor learn from his mistakes. It sometimes takes a serious crisis to bring him to himself, when he can see his life for what it is. In the meantime, he may have shortchanged himself and the others he has influenced with his dead-end-street philosophy.

Several girls waiting to have their babies in a home for unmarried mothers were discussing what advice they would give young people who were still virgins. Here are some of the things they said:

1st girl:
"I advise the girls to stay virgins."

2nd girl:
"And if they aren't, to stop all activities that can cause them to get into trouble."

1st girl:
"Try to control their emotions. Try to keep a level head even though it is a very difficult thing to do. You don't realize how hard it is until you get yourself involved in a situation."

3rd girl:
"I didn't believe I'd ever get this far. . ."

4th girl:
"That's just it. I think everybody thinks 'I can stop' and 'I know when it's time to stop,' but then you get so far and you just don't realize, and then all of a sudden, it's just plain all over. . . . You're not really thinking too straight right then, you know. We know we absolutely shouldn't have done it and all that, but at the time, when you are emotionally involved you don't sit up and think, 'Should I or shouldn't I? What's good and what's bad about it?' He says, 'I love you . . . if you love me . . .' and you say, 'I love you but,' and well, go on and you're lost. . . . You should just say, 'If you love me, you won't ask me to.' "

Over and over again one hears girls and fellows say they thought they could stop but found that they could not.

Control Is Part of Life

No one can let his feelings run wild, doing just what he pleases all the time. As you mature, you have to learn how to control yourself in order to live with others. When you were young, your parents controlled your behavior. Now it is up to you to manage yourself. This is true of all aspects of your life. Your self-control is an important part of your personality—in managing your time, budgeting your money, getting along with your friends, and governing your sex behavior.

There is no evidence that self-control hurts your sex life. Quite the contrary tends to be true. As you learn to control your sexual feelings, they become ever more meaningful and satisfying. It is the fellow or the girl who goes around with his emotions all unbuttoned who is in the greatest danger. The self-controlled person can bear to wait. He learns what is appropriate not only for the situation but for his own life. He refrains from doing those things that will harm himself and others. He keeps his powers within those bounds that are an asset rather than a liability for him and for those he cares about.

This is so in many areas of life. Electricity, for instance, is a great natural force. But, running wild as lightning, it can burn down a building in a great blazing holocaust. It can ruin in a few minutes what has taken years to build and develop. It can, and often does, destroy that which is most precious to man and nature. Yet lightning is "natural," uncontrolled, electric power. That same energy through the wires of your home can provide light and heat for years. Electricity under control can cook your food, warm your home in winter and cool it in summer, bring in the magic of radio and television, and keep the wheels of industry whirring through the years.

Sex, like electricity, can run wild and out of control. Or properly channeled, it, too, can light and heat your life through the years. It can destroy others, hurt your loved ones, and damage your children, or it can bless all who have anything to do with you. Yet it is still sex—the kind of power that, like love, makes the world go around.

People used to think that sex was bad, because of all the harm it did. They became ashamed of having sexual feelings. They hid their bodies and refused to talk about their sex interests. The day of such prudery and hypocrisy has passed, fortunately.

Now we are going through a great revolution in which some people are going to the other extreme and insisting that all sex is good. Actually, sex is good, and healthy, and satisfying only when it is appropriately controlled. Sex that is not wisely controlled can wreck your life. Under control, it can be a positive power for all that means most to a man, a woman, and their children.

Saying that sex is either good or bad is like saying that paint is one or the other. Paint splashed in hate on a synagogue door is bad. But that same paint in the hands of a Leonardo da Vinci is good through the centuries in the eyes of all who behold it. The difference is not in the pigment. The crux of the matter is in the way it is used.

You are learning that sex is natural. It is a God-given part of you. It is not to be denied. Whatever you do with it, it still will be there. You can throw it away and yourself with it, if you wish. Or you can learn to manage it, like the man or woman you aspire to be. Your sex life will be as good or as bad as you make it. No more, no less. Express it casually, as a simple biological hunger, and you go emotionally hungry as a person. Treat it as a reflex, and all you have is a simple release of tension. See it as the most intimate way in which two persons can merge their lives, and you find meaning that is deep and lasting. One of the tragedies of taking sexual relations cheaply is that you miss out on the rich fulfillment that sex in a loving marriage brings.

Norman Vincent Peale puts this point succinctly when he writes:

> Sex in the right place and the right time with the right person under the right circumstances is a magnificent thing. But almost by definition this means sex under the seal and shield of marriage. Under any other circumstances it is likely to be clumsy, guilt-ridden and spiritually enervating ... Sexual restraint does not mean deprivations; it means happiness in depth.

4. It's Fun—Always?

Some people have the idea that sex is nothing but fun, fun, fun. The torrid pictures you have seen suggest that utter bliss is found in sexual relationships. The sexy stories you have heard imply that you, too, will always find ecstasy in the arms of your lover. Popular songs come right out and tell you that this is the friendliest thing two people can do. Young people around you imply you have not lived until you have proven yourself sexually.

It is true that sex can be lots of fun. Given a devoted husband and wife, a sense of security, and an appropriate setting, and sex life can bring deeply meaningful pleasure. But the right conditions are not always present, especially for unmarried teen-agers. Therefore, the sex act itself is no guarantee of fun.

It's Not Fun If You Don't Enjoy It

Premarital sex experience is often anything but enjoyable. There are several reasons why going all the way before marriage frequently brings more pain than pleasure.

1. *First sex experiences are often disappointing.* The fellow becomes too excited too quickly. He may appear impotent or unable to sustain an erection long enough at first. It takes time for a girl to awaken sexually before she, too, can respond. She must become gradually accustomed to sexual activity before she finds it even comfortable. The physical act between two partners who move at different tempos is frequently unpleasant. The married couple develop their own harmony as they each learn and teach one another the language of love, in time. But such "music" is rare at first.

The male approaches sex experience with his attention focused on the two bodies and their behavior. He is aware of the activity within his sex organs and concentrates on his functioning as a male. His sexual response to girls is first of all to the female body. In time he gradually learns to love one special person for herself. But this takes time, and tenderness, and mutual devotion.

A girl gives herself to her sweetheart because she loves him and wants to please him. She needs his assurance and acceptance and encouragement in order to feel lovable. She comes to sex experience with her primary attention on how her lover makes her feel. She responds to the attention he shows her. When he is rough and urgent, it is hard for her to respond normally. She is completely his only when he awakens in her the readiness for completion.

Boys tend to be body-centered, and girls are person-centered from the first. Thus, their premarital experiences can be frustrating. The boy may go through with it, but without the satisfaction her response would have brought him. The girl may attempt to match his enthusiasm, but be left unsatisfied, unawakened, or uneasy. Both the boy and the girl looking for a significant relationship risk losing it or never finding it in the premarital affair.

2. *Adequacy as male and female* is hard to establish in premarital sex experience. Dr. Flanders Dunbar reminds us that teenagers know that a rule is being broken when they go all the way before marriage. This fact interferes with their communication as partners. Because each feels a little anxious and a little guilty, the girl is likely to be frigid and the boy at least partially impotent. They may be left with the feeling that they are inadequate human beings when the very thing they set out to prove was their competence.

There are young people today who are driven to test their virility and maturity through sex. They are afraid of being inadequate. But what they do is only to increase their haunting fear that somehow they do not measure up. The boy feels that he is to blame for the girl's lack of genuine response. The girl who gave in to the boy as the price she felt she had to pay for his attention, all too often feels cheated, and that the cost was too great. She hoped to hold him with sex, but she feels devalued and disillusioned when he turns from her as soon as he finds the girl he wants to marry.

3. *Sex alone is not a strong bond.* It is widely recognized that some fellows are active sexually with "bad" girls even while they are going with "good" girls. While they respect their sweethearts and are willing to wait for marriage before insisting upon sex experience with them, they relieve their sex drives with the kind of girl they would not consider marrying. Pick-ups are not hard to find. Their reputations spread like wildfire among all kinds of fellows. Dr. Ehrmann reports that the "easy make" is found in larger numbers in high schools than on college campuses. Some fellows say that they engage in a group-type of sexual experience with such girls in high school. These contacts are momentary and transitory. The promiscuous girl has no hold on the men with whom she consorts. They are literally here tonight and gone tomorrow. There is no bond of loyalty or sense of unity in this kind of sex experience.

If there are personal feelings at all, they are likely to be of revulsion and relief once the physical act is over.

An impersonal attitude toward sex partners is common. Dr. Kinsey found that the overwhelming tendency of sexually promiscuous women was to feel callous and complacent about their behavior. They have more sex affairs before and after they marry. But they find less meaning in them. It is the familiar refrain of having more but enjoying it less.

The prostitute or call girl is sexually most active. She is convenient, available, and undemanding. She requires no wooing skill or personal attractiveness of the man. She takes one partner after another without feeling or commitment beyond the fee. She and the man who buys her time risk more than meaning in a loveless act. Their contact is in conflict with the law, in danger of underworld involvements, theft, blackmail, and venereal infection. Sex alone has no tie except to trouble.

Two out of three premarital experiences are casual contacts. Dr. Kirkendall interprets this by saying that almost any boy who wants to can get a prostitute or pick-up. Sex with affection takes time and attention to develop, and therefore it is more rare.

4. *Personal communication is central in sexual fulfillment.* The better the couple know each other, and the more communication they have before their sex experience, the more emotionally meaningful it is. Dr. Kirkendall reports that experience in intercourse itself does not make communication easier. A number of the couples that he interviewed said they had no personal communication at all after they began to have premarital intercourse.

It takes time for a boy and girl to get through to one another as persons. If they rush into sexual activity, they run the risk of cutting off their chances of getting to know and love one another as persons. When that happens, even their sex life lacks the possibility of fulfillment, because it is not founded upon personal communication Before they are ready for intimacy, they must find one another as two human beings with dreams, aspirations, and feelings. This mutual discovery is a delightful experience in itself. As two persons reveal more and more of their secret selves to one another, they develop a strong sense of unity. They feel that they belong to each other. They have built a bond of communication that provides a solid foundation for physical union. Without that personal ability to get through to each other as two whole personalities, their sex union can be superficial and unrewarding. Sex without love is apt to be a negative experience.

5. *Guilt is a real possibility.* There are couples who report that they have no feelings of guilt at having sex experience before marriage. Some engaged couples that Professors Burgess and Wallin studied said they had no regrets at having had each other sexually. They felt that what they did was their own business. They were sure of each other, and certain that what they did was right for them.

There is no doubt that other people suffer serious guilt feelings from having gone all the way before marriage. They feel guilty that they have not done the right thing. They are torn within themselves for having gone beyond their own standards. Guilt, recriminations, and blame often go together. One young woman says, for instance:

> . . . I came back to reality with a sickening thud. I wasn't drunk any more. Nothing was funny now. The party was over and I felt sick, cheap, and dirty. It didn't make me feel any better to hear him say, "Why on earth didn't you stop us before things went too far? You should have known what would happen. You could have called a halt any time. But you didn't."

Guilt feelings are most frequent among those with high moral standards. Young people who have grown up in good homes are apt to feel guilty when they do something they have been taught is wrong. Professor Christensen compared young people from permissive cultures such as in Denmark with religiously oriented young people in the United States. He found American young people much more guilty about premarital sex than are Danish youth.

The evidence is clear that guilt feelings are a real possibility for sexually active teen-agers whose families expect chastity of them. Church young people usually have such strong consciences that they cannot feel right about doing something they have been brought up to believe is wrong. Fortunately, these young people are less likely than others to indulge in premarital sex experience. They tend to feel more sure of their standards and live up to them without too much stress or strain.

6. *Fear of discovery* keeps many an unmarried couple from full enjoyment of their intimacy. Because it is generally considered wrong, the boy and girl approach each other with anxiety. Their ears are alert for any possible witness to their indiscretion. Their attention cannot be entirely upon each other, so long as they are afraid of being caught. Even if what they are doing has gone undetected so far, there is always the danger that somehow someone will find out. This fear of being discovered may add an exciting sense of mischief, a challenge to authority, a defiance of rules, or

rebellion. Often it is accompanied by so much anxiety that one or both members of the pair fails to enjoy their intimate activity.

One girl who has already submitted to her boy friend says, "You have guilt feelings. . . .You think that everybody knows or he's told his friends and his friends have told their friends and all the kids. You just shrivel up in front of them. You're afraid to say anything."

Some boys do kiss and tell. A girl has reason to doubt the sincerity of her lover when she finds that he has been bragging of his conquest. He may need to bolster up his ego by telling the other fellows of what he has done. Sometimes a lovers' quarrel over trivialities precipitates a spiteful exposé. Revenge is a further motive as a previously intimate association becomes strained.

As soon as an intimate relationship is discovered, both members of the pair can be hurt. The girl is teased by some girls and avoided by others. Or, even worse, she is propositioned by the wilder boys when she gets the label "easy." Occasionally a fellow who thought he was safe finds the girls he used to know snubbing him or giggling as he passes by. He knows without their saying a word that what he thought was private has become public information.

7. *The need for concealment* of premarital sexual intercourse gives little or no security to the relationship. The couple has to sneak off in ways designed to deceive. The clandestine contact has to be stealthy to come off at all. The pair plot their coming together in some secret time and place that they hope will escape notice. They watch for moments when their intimacy will have at least some semblance of privacy, even in a public setting.

The thrill of forbidden fruit is like a small boy's enjoyment of stolen apples. More mature couples find that the stealthy quality of their contact makes them feel cheap. The relationship of even the most devoted pair seems shabby when it must be shrouded in secrecy. Lovers usually want to tell the world how they feel. But this is rarely possible in premarital affairs.

8. *Haste is a risk* for many an unmarried couple. Pleasure in sexual intimacy requires a sense of leisure all too often lacking before marriage. A man and wife can look forward to long, quiet evenings together. They can take the time for the mutual loving and being loved that bring fulfillment to them both. They can prepare for their coming together with all the pleasant accompaniments that make their relationship throb with significance. Soft music, their favorite scents, special arrangements that heighten their pleasure in each other can be arranged in advance. Their lovemaking is in their own bed, amidst surroundings that they have

lovingly prepared. A married couple's sex life can be richly varied and full of ritual because they have time to develop a repertoire of response to one another. Dr. LeMon Clark advises married couples:

> Real sexual adjustment can come about in marriage only when a couple feel free to work toward such an end. They must free themselves from all sense of sin and guilt regarding sexual actions and activity. They must be willing to take time out to enjoy it. They must not put off attempts at intercourse until they are under such tension that they cannot take time to get the greatest amount of pleasurable experience from it.

The young pair before marriage all too often have to snatch what they can get where they can get it. Their contact is suffused with urgency. The girl, and often the boy, too, is left unsatisfied even after having gone through the motions of going all the way.

9. *Being exploited is no fun.* One of the disillusioning aspects of premarital sex for the girl is feeling that she simply has been used for the boy's pleasure. An attractive girl who has been going with a popular college boy tells of her disillusionment at finding that she is "just a body" to him. She has recently discovered that he has a girl with whom he consorts regularly in each of several communities. The feeling she had for him when she thought her love was reciprocated abruptly disappeared when she learned she was only one of several. She says she is not willing to be just another female for him. Not only is he no fun for her anymore, but she remembers nothing pleasant about the times they have been together. It all is "a big vulgar mess," which she will not continue, and yet cannot quite forget. She is ashamed of it all. Sex was not fun for her. One cannot help but wonder whether the boy who caused her humiliation looks back upon his relations with her with real pleasure.

10. *Uneven commitment is not funny.* One of the differences between the sexes is that sexual relations tend to make the female more possessive of her man. She tends to become more emotionally involved with her sex partner than he does with her. Once premarital sex is underway, the girl urges permanence and "getting things settled." But it is when she becomes too demanding that he is most likely to want to regain his freedom.

One of the most frequent questions teen-age boys ask is, "How can I get my girl back in circulation? She has given me the best months of her life. But I've had it. How can I let her down easy?" Many years ago, Dr. Willard Waller recognized this as the principle of uneven commitment. The one who is most involved is most easily hurt when the relationship breaks. The girl is the more likely of the two to feel that she and her partner belong to one another once they have established sexual relations. Therefore she presses for marriage about the time the fellow is through with her.

Even if she is not too demanding, the boy still may feel obligated. One fellow put it this way:

> I felt very obligated to continue the relationship because of her fine reputation, and I think this obligation caused plenty of inner tension on my part. Her fear of pregnancy and the probable loss of self-respect upset her a great deal. Her menstrual cycle was upset. She felt very guilty about the experiences . . . It had come too soon, and we weren't ready for it.

The unpleasant side effects of premarital sexual relations are not funny to either the girl or the fellow. Doctors report that such symptoms as depression, ennui, inability to study, to sleep, or to eat often accompany the turmoil of uneasy love. It piles up so heavily that the relationship between two compatible sweethearts can break under the strain. This is one reason why so many devoted couples break their engagements rather than go on into marriage. They did not know the effect their intimacy would have on their relationship until it was too late. They get in too deep, too fast, and then cannot go through with their plans. They separate, and each tries to put the pieces of life together. Dr. Paul Walters, Jr., Harvard psychiatrist, finds that when a woman does not find the fidelity she seeks from her lover, she either retreats from sexuality, or she considers herself promiscuous—neither a pleasant possibility.

Being Sexy Is Not All Fun

Some girls attract men as a flower attracts bees. They have the kind of come-on that arouses men's desire. Other girls may envy the attention they get, without realizing that being sexy has its price.

Marilyn Monroe once said that a sex symbol becomes a thing, and she hated being a thing. She was a sex symbol for millions. But she found that "people took a lot for granted, not only could they be friendly, but they could suddenly get overly friendly and expect an awful lot for very little." What happens to our sex symbols? Marilyn Monroe ended up naked and alone, with an empty bottle of sleeping pills beside a silent telephone. Her beautiful body lay unclaimed at the county morgue—a tragic end to a tragic life. Being sexy can be exciting for a while. But the girl who bases her life upon her sexual attractiveness has little but loneliness and heartbreak ahead. If she weathers the stormy years of men's desire and other women's envy, she grows old enough to lose her youthful appeal and has little left to take its place.

The fellow who has a reputation for being a wolf does not "have it made" either. He fails to win the admiration of the kind of girl he would like to marry when he is ready to settle down. He experiences a kind of emotional insensitivity and superficiality. In time any woman is like all the others he has known. Not knowing any one really well, he actually knows none at all. Once having broken with respectability, his attitudes and behavior become more and more nonconformist and irresponsible.

One such fellow sadly told of his unsuccessful attempts to woo an attractive girl. He had played around so long that he did not know how to love her with tenderness. She actually had laughed at his clumsy efforts. His approach to women had always been so rough that he had no idea of how to love the girl he wanted to marry. Professor Ehrmann could have told him that men are usually more aggressive with casual partners than with the girls they love. Unfortunately, too few fellows or girls know that being sexy is not always and forever enjoyable—for either sex.

You today are surrounded with sexual stimulation. The newsstands are filled with bright-colored magazines and paperbacks that are designed to be sexually exciting. One family doctor tells of a fourteen-year-old girl patient of his who brought him a copy of a girlie magazine lavish with pictures. She showed him three separate spreads in which nationally known entertainers were pictured in a series of sexual encounters that left little to the imagination. The incidents were described with a raw humor that made it all sound like good rowdy sport. The teen-age girl asked her doctor what she should do when this kind of picture was passed around her crowd. She was especially concerned because her boy friend enjoyed this kind of thing, and still he seemed like a nice fellow in other ways. The doctor explained that teen-age boys more than girls find sexy pictures stimulating sexually. One reason why fellows go for "dirty" post cards and stories is for the sexy kicks they give.

Many a fellow who does not really want to get involved in the rough talk of other boys finds it hard to pull out when the other guys get started. The dirty stories are accompanied by the raucous laughter and knowing winks that make him feel "out" if he does not go along with the crowd. When the shady sallies are exchanged in front of their girl friends, the boys sometimes get too excited to behave. Then the situation is hard to handle by the young persons who do not want to get involved in sex play. Sensible young people learn to slip out of such sex-toned situations without making a scene. They find it better to "have another engagement" than to be losers in the game of sex.

Drinking and Illicit Sex

Sex and drinking go together in mixed company. When the fuse is touched off with alcohol, it is sometimes too short to stop in time. Dr. Celia Deschin found girls reporting that their first sexual relations occurred when they were under the influence of drink. The bottle did not start it, but it made it easier to go through with. A teen-age boy and girl can wake up with a hang-over and ugly memories of sordid sex after a drinking bout. Alcohol numbs one's judgment and lulls a person into behavior that would have been unthinkable without the drinks. As a fellow said not long ago, "If I hadn't gotten so drunk, I wouldn't be in this mess. I'm not the kind of guy to foul up a nice girl like I did. But after too many drinks I just wasn't myself at all."

The wolf has no such scruples. One fast worker says:

I only date a girl who "puts out." In the beginning of the evening we go for a car ride and drink. If my date gets drunk, it's all the better, as she doesn't know what she's doing. Before I ask a girl for a date, I have to meet her and see if she has a good figure. I'm not going to waste my time and money on a girl who won't make me feel real good while I'm on her.

There is a point of view that says, "What is moral is what you feel good after." The catch is—"How soon after?" A fellow may feel fine after a few drinks and a session with a girl. But his feelings the next day, or a few months later, may be anything but fine, and the price may come high. Looking at premarital sex entirely from a fun point of view, you have to admit that any interlude of pleasure has within it the possibility of pain. No behavior is unalloyed pleasure. As philosophers have long recognized, when the fun-lover cannot get what he wants, he is restless and dissatisfied. When he gets what he wants, he becomes bored. The life of the pleasure-seeker swings from pain to boredom and from boredom to pain with little real fun in it.

J. B. Priestley reminds us that eroticism is a trap into which more and more young moderns are falling. They are not finding fuller lives and richer relationships, but only barren titillation. For eroticism in itself, wanting a sensation and not another person, makes love impossible.

5 If You Are Really In Love—Why Not?

*T*wo young people can care so much for each other that they actually feel married long before they reach the altar. Is acting as though they are husband and wife all right for them? Are there reasons why feeling in love is *not* enough to justify going all the way before marriage? These are difficult questions for many a fellow and girl. Yet each individual, every couple, must find workable answers for how far they will go in expressing their love for one another.

Some lovers go the limit before marriage and have few regrets about what they have done. Others feel so guilty and ashamed of their premarital sex experience that their relationship is seriously damaged—sometimes to the breaking point. How can you tell how you would feel about going all the way with your sweetheart? You can't. Sex experience is so highly charged emotionally, especially with a person you love, that it is almost impossible to predict how you and your partner will feel.

How others say they feel after they have gone all the way is not the most reliable index of how you might feel about the same experience. It does not even indicate clearly how they themselves actually react. They may have a very temporary feeling of unity that may or may not last. They may rationalize what they have done in an effort to justify their behavior. Boasting about how much in love they are is most usual among those who have yet to find real and lasting love. True love for another person has a personal quality that does not flaunt itself. That is why the couple who are deeply in love are not so obvious in their love-making as are the pair whose love is not based upon mutual respect and consideration.

What Do You Gain, What Do You Lose?

If you go all the way with your beloved before marriage, what might you gain? The boy gets the immediate release of sexual tensions, with the girl he loves. The girl may get a sense of being desired and desirable in the eyes of her sweetheart. They both can let themselves go without the restraint needed to keep their love-making within conventional bounds. They get to test their compatability, at least at the time, before they go on into marriage. They may find that their love is stronger than ever for having been expressed sexually before marriage.

For every possible gain, however, there is a possible loss. The boy may or may not love and respect his sweetheart for having gone all the way before marriage. He may find that his feelings for his sweetheart are no longer so intense now that he has had her sexually. He may feel dissatisfaction arising from the clandestine nature of their coming together. He may worry about getting her into trouble. Perhaps he fears that she is trapping him into marriage before he is ready to go through with it. It is possible that he feels guilty about taking advantage of his sweetheart's love, especially if she had been a virgin.

The girl may feel desirable, or she may feel shabby for having overstepped the bounds of chastity with her lover. She may experience great mental conflict and regret over what she has done, as some of Dr. Kinsey's subjects did. Even though she submitted to what her sweetheart wanted of her, she may fear that he ultimately will reject her. A goodly percentage of American men want to marry virgins—a tendency that many a girl has found in her own experience. She loves her man and gives in to his insistence, only to find that by so doing she loses him in time to some girl who would not permit such liberties. Whether or not this particular boy will behave this way, a girl may fear that he will, and has no way of knowing ahead of time what his, or her, reactions will be.

The couple may lose the excitement that restraint brings to a relationship. One couple have gone steady for a long while. They feel genuine love for one another. For some months now they have been sleeping together several times a week. Now they both report that the glow has gone, and they are at the point of breaking up. She feels cheated that all he wants to do is "eat and fall into bed together." She misses the long, quiet chats on the sofa that used to bring such a close sense of companionship. He complains that she nags him "just like an old married woman." He finds her less attractive now that he knows her intimately. He has even convinced himself that "if she would do it with me, she might do it with anyone."

Happily married couples take a considerable period of time to work out a mutually satisfying sexual adjustment, as Dr. Landis found. How then, is a period of premarital testing a reliable gauge of a couple's compatibility? It takes not only time, but a feeling of permanence, security, and belonging together to bring many a woman to full sexual awakening. It takes a feeling of being married in the fullest sense to make sex completely meaningful to both the husband and the wife.

Too early sexual involvement can blind a pair to the other important aspects of their relationship that they should be building as a sound foundation for their marriage. All too often they "fall into bed," rather than talk out the many things that should be shared and discussed. Once sexual intercourse starts, their interpersonal communication slackens off in many a case. Thus, in their coming together the couple may lose the very thing they sought to ensure—intimacy and companionship as a pair.

Premarital sex between lovers is often hounded by the question, "But if you really love me, why can't we be married?" If the boy is not ready to get married, he can feel too pushed by the girl's insistence on getting things settled. He interprets her demands for marriage as "nagging," and finds himself avoiding her, as men so often withdraw when their women become too demanding. At times it is the girl who does not want to be pushed into marriage by an insistent lover. She may be quite content to let things drift while she finishes her education and enjoys not being too tied down. Her refusal to "make it legal" may baffle her lover, who may have too easily assumed that intimacy is *the* way to sweep a girl into matrimony.

With so many negative possibilities in premarital sexual relations between lovers, it is not surprising that so many intimate pairs break up rather than go on into marriage. They may separate with a mutual sense of relief. They may both be badly hurt by what they have done to one another. Or the one who is the more involved emotionally may undergo a severe emotional shock at the loss of the loved one.

The greater the personal investment in the relationship, the greater the chance of being hurt when it breaks. Scars from unsuccessful love affairs can make a person bitter or overly sensitive. She carries a torch for her falsehearted lover and allows no other man close enough to rescue her. He becomes cynical about women and loses his capacity to love again with the intensity he once knew. One or the other may rebound into another affair that bears the burden of the previous failure.

Lovers' Double Danger

The danger of premarital sexual relations between lovers is a weakening of their feeling for one another on the one hand, and the possibility of being hurt by too great involvement on the other. Waiting until marriage before starting to live together as man and wife circumvents both these dangers. When the honeymoon is over in marriage, the two are still tied in mutually dependent roles that make for permanence. They have a baby and reinforce each other as mother and father. They have a home to keep and a life to live that goes beyond romance and sexual response alone. The more involved they become, the more their marriage means to them both. There is always the risk of losing that which you love, but the risk is far less in marriage than it is for unmarried lovers.

Professor Robert O. Blood, Jr., speaking of love before marriage, says, "when a couple chooses to 'go all the way,' it should be prepared for the possibility that the romantic bubble may collapse in the process." The sense of mystery in which each views the other is shattered by their physical intimacy. Their romantic interest in one another may slacken off once they have gone the limit. The idealization that mobilizes couples for marriage is greatly diminished by sex experience.

The noted psychoanalyst Dr. Theodor Reik says that frustration-born idealization of women is necessary for their achievement and maintenance of a status above the animal level. When sex is delayed until marriage, lovers concentrate on the personal and social qualities of one another. In fact, love that transcends physical passion wells up when attention is focused on the whole personality of the beloved, *before* the sexual relation is consummated in marriage. Premarital chastity can strengthen the respect and love between two sweethearts that lead to the full expression of both personalities within the marriage.

Many a girl recognizes these things, too late. Professor Shipman reports about a girl's sober second thoughts, "When I look back, I think it might have been because of a fear of losing the fellow I was going with. He was the first boy I really fell in love with. . . . Maybe I let it happen in hopes he would fall in love with me as much as I fell for him."

He was the first boy she fell in love with, but will he be the last? Probably not. Most girls, and fellows, fall in love a number of times through their teen years. This is not because they are fickle. They are not necessarily falsehearted lovers. They may feel that they are genuinely in love, at the time. For throughout the second decade of life a young person is discovering his, or her, own emotional potential.

You may be in love now. You probably will be again, perhaps

several times, before you find the person you eventually marry. Right now you are discovering the kinds of persons you like. With each one you feel different. The chances are that you never will love any two persons in exactly the same way. Each individual you know brings out a different facet of your own personality.

Right now you are developing your emotional repertoire in relation to members of the other sex. You are learning all the forms that love can take as you feel them in interaction with the persons you become fond of in different ways. With one you feel silly; with another, serious. With one beloved person you feel tender and nurturing; with another, all hot and bothered with sexy excitement. One sweetheart may be a pal; another, too glamorous to touch or talk with much.

In time, you not only get experience in the kinds of persons that most appeal to you, but also you become able to appraise your own love feelings. You say to yourself, "She's quite a dish. I could go for her sexually, but I would hate to live with her very long." Or you think, "He is slow, but he is solid and gives me a sense of security that I need with the man of my life." You learn to recognize what you need most in a temporary companion, and in a life mate. You sense that your own feelings are a good guide to love, as soon as you can interpret them correctly.

Miracle of Sudden Intimacy

Falling in love is a miracle of sudden intimacy. It hits you when you are least prepared for it. Suddenly, there, across a crowded room, is a laugh, a smile, an attraction that cannot be questioned. What is it that draws you so magnetically together? It is often initiated by sex appeal and attraction, which may or may not grow into a lasting love relationship. Sudden falling in love is sometimes with an individual who in an unrecognized way reminds you of some past affection. Something about that special person reminds you, often without your being aware of it, of someone who once meant a great deal to you. It may have been a favorite relative whom you adored as a child. It may have been a former sweetheart whom you loved "not wisely but too well." It could be almost anything in your emotional make-up that causes you to respond so quickly to a stranger.

Then how can you know whether it will last and blossom into a real love? You can't. It may, or it may not, depending upon the two of you as persons and how much you have to share with one another as a couple. How can you manage your own love feelings for someone you know is an unlikely lover? You face them for what they are, and stop kidding yourself that because you love him or her, you have to do something about it.

Elise is a good example of what we are talking about. She has just taken a summer job with a cleaning establishment, before going into nurse's training in the fall. She says:

> My problem is: I have fallen in love with a married man. He is one of our route drivers. He is around twenty-eight, and has been married for five years. He has a nice wife, and a wonderful son, two years old. My love for him is so deep, that I cannot seem to understand its depths. His character is so very outstanding. He has an instinctive strut and born dashing appeal. He is a born leader. He has the respect of all who know him, and whoever was fortunate to come in contact with him. I find myself so hopelessly in love with him. He is not what one may call handsome, as a matter of fact he is about a head shorter than myself. What his physical looks are, makes no difference to me. What I feel for him, has a warm mellow glow, which delves so deep, so very deep.
>
> His marriage is not one of the best, but he abides by it. I wish with all my heart that it could be myself who is his wife. I am not jealous of his wife. I couldn't be. But, I know that she is a very fortunate woman. As for his getting a divorce and my marrying him—well—that can never be. But, I love him very much and always will in some small way.
>
> How can I break the hurt that I feel so often? I know where the heart is concerned, every love has a meaning. But, what can I do? How can I control the love that I feel?

The very act of facing up to the impossibility of anything coming of her feelings for the man was a necessary first step for Elise to take. In time, she came to realize what it was about the fellow that made her respond so warmly to him. She was wise enough to do nothing that would threaten his wife's place in his life, or that would risk hurting herself with a hopeless affair with a married man. By the time she was well into nurse's training, she could look back with amusement on this early "infatuation," as she called it as soon as she got over it.

This is one characteristic of a good many early love affairs—you get over them. You may feel very much in love. You may feel that what you have with each other is so genuine and meaningful that it will last forever. But it does not, as often as not. You get over it, whatever it was. And next year, or the year after, you wonder what it was that so attracted you to such a person. What it was, you may never know completely. But you can know that love feelings alone are not enough to justify complete commitment.

Dr. Erich Fromm points out in his book *The Art of Loving* that love is indeed an art. As the musician makes real music only after he has mastered the theory and the practice required of him as an artist, so each of us must learn to love. As a doctor must undergo the discipline of years of learning the details of the art of medicine, so you must give yourself to learning the meaning and expression of love in your life. This means learning to give and to care for and to assume responsibility for your love and your loved one. For "love is possible only if two persons communicate with each other from the center of their existence."

This does not come suddenly. The ability truly to love and be loved is learned through the years. Too early focus of love feelings in sexual intercourse cuts off the ability to love deeply and broadly as human beings can. It is so that they may learn to love that a couple postpones complete intimacy until they are ready—as persons, and as a pair.

So What Do You Do, When You Love One Another?

What do you do when you love one another? You do not have to *do* anything. You may be in love now, as you have been before, and as you will be again. But that does not mean that you must express all this warmth sexually. Just being drawn to another person is not sufficient reason for physical intimacy.

Love requires neither sex nor marriage for satisfaction. Unless you go in for serial polygamy, you do not rush to get married every time you are attracted to a member of the other sex. Hopping into bed with every individual you feel fond of would be ridiculous, if not downright immoral. You keep yourself free to love and to be loved by many, many persons of both sexes, either married or unmarried, when you reserve your sex life for your marriage partner.

Of course you will love the one you marry. The one thing that will make this married love unique through the years is that it alone is expressed sexually. Saving sex for marriage gives you something very special to share with one another, which no one else can have. Into your married love, then, you can pour all your feelings as husband and wife, co-partners in building a marriage and family together.

Love then becomes a universal possibility to be developed widely without danger of harming your life plans or your beloved friends' family life. You can dare to love beyond marriage only when the threat of sexuality is removed from your non-marital associations.

Keeping sex for marriage protects you from others' exploitation. The British author J. B. Priestley reminds us that the lover is ready to give everything, all that is of value in his life. This makes a loving person vulnerable to "being used" by any unscrupulous person "on the make" unless sex is carefully regulated.

Premarital chastity safeguards you from deceiving yourself unwittingly. The danger is that you fall in love with someone who is not really there at all. You become bewitched by the magic of your own unconscious depths. Thus, you do not really see your beloved for what he or she actually is. When you feel lonely, rejected, or neglected (possibly with good cause), you are at the mercy of your own neurotic needs. You may convince yourself you are in love, when you are just licking your wounds. What you are calling "love" can be merely an escape from your problems.

You can avoid being trapped into going further in the intimate expression of your feelings by taking such practical safeguards as:

1. Becoming aware of your own lonely, rebellious, and love-hungry needs, and devising acceptable ways of getting back on an even keel emotionally without letting your feelings trick you into behavior you will regret later

2. Avoiding the fast workers and the loose company, whose moral standards are not your own

3. Keeping out of the compromising situations where you may not be able to cope with the consequences. Being alone together in the privacy of a bedroom in a house, motel, or hotel, or the back seat of a car may be more temptation than either of you can manage

4. Recognizing that drinking and prolonged petting and erotic movies and risqué talk are all stage-setters for going further sexually than you may have intended

5. Respecting the urgency of the sex urge in yourself and others, enough to keep from being rushed pell-mell into going all the way until *you* decide you are ready

6. Participating in all sorts of activities while you are together —sports and music, trips and service projects, group fun and twosome discussions—so that you will not be caught in long periods of being together without anything to do

7. Being wary of going steady or getting engaged until you are really sure; then making plans for marriage when you are truly ready without the hazards of the too short or the too long engagement

8. Cultivating many ways of saying "I love you" without having to depend upon close physical intimacy for being or feeling loved

As you head toward marriage with the one you feel you want to belong to the rest of your life, you want to express your love—in a wide variety of special ways. You enjoy developing together a rich repertoire of love rituals that become a special language between you two. Agreeing that you want to wait until marriage before beginning your sex life, you free yourselves for the multi-faceted courtship that is difficult to establish once you start living together as husband and wife.

The fellow who tenderly cherishes his sweetheart as though she were someone very special is learning the ways of love that mean much to a girl of any age. The girl who learns to listen when her sweetheart speaks, to feel compassion and sweetness in her relationship with him is laying a good foundation for being a wife and mother. The couple who meet each other's eyes with empathy, knowing without words what the other is thinking or feeling, find meanings of "the two shall be one" in spirit that becomes flesh after marriage. The lovers who learn to talk with one another about all sorts of things build a foundation for communication through their marriage. The sweethearts who come to share how they truly feel about their innermost dreams and disappointments develop a companionship basis for a full and complete life together after they marry.

What you do with your beloved is up to you. You may express your feelings in whatever ways make sense to you. Just do not kid yourself or each other, that you cannot really enjoy each other except through sexual intercourse. If that is the case, then what you have may be sexual attraction rather than real love for one another. What you do as sweethearts reflects the kinds of persons you are, your relationship with one another, and the life you see ahead for yourselves.

6 Is Sexual Restraint

Is sexual restraint bad for you? The answer is a simple "No." It does not hurt you to inhibit your sexual feelings. Restraining sexual impulses harms neither males nor females, old wives' tales notwithstanding. Boys are not hurt by managing their erotic drives. They are not necessarily any healthier for having gone all the way. Girls are no prettier for having given themselves sexually. In fact, your ability to manage your impulses is an essential part of your health as a person. Inhibitions do not necessarily make you nervous. If what you are doing makes sense to you, you can wait— as you do in almost every other area of life—until it is right for you to "express yourself." You are in much greater danger of becoming a nervous wreck when you feel guilty about your behavior, as many a psychiatrist can tell you.

Dr. Carl Binger, psychiatric consultant to the Harvard University Medical Services, points out that a girl needs a man she can respect if she is to feel secure. Having the love of a young fellow she admires seems the safest bulwark for her own self-doubt. But she soon finds that the young fellows her age are often less ready for a rewarding and growing relationship than she is. Her tower of strength may turn out to be a slender reed at best. Then she may go into a tail spin or a depression. This college doctor finds girls who have expected too much of their men plagued by such symptoms as loss of zest, feelings of apathy, fatigue, an apparent need for extra hours of sleep, a very much lowered self-esteem, and most of all by an inability to get their work done.

The girl who is worried about the tormenting question, "What will happen to me?" has difficulty paying attention in class. She finds it hard to concentrate, and to understand what she hears and reads. She broods. She daydreams, and becomes more and more dissatisfied with herself. She feels guilty about the time and opportunities she is wasting. She thinks to herself, "I must not let my parents down. Sending me through school has not been easy for them." She says, "I can't understand it. I always have been a good student. Why, year before last I was third in my class." And so she goes, around and around in her own anxiety about herself.

A recent scholarly report, *The Character of Danger,* finds no evidence that sexual frustration is a prime factor in the development of problems. In fact, the researchers find the highest prevalence of

Bad For You?

nervous symptoms among those with the least sexual restraint.

Your Development as a Person

The free-love advocates would have you believe that sublimating your sex drive is bad for you. But experts of stature agree that sublimation is important for your development as a person. Anna Freud defines sublimation as the process of sexual and aggressive energy being displaced by nonsexual and nondestructive goals. She reminds us of how personal experience in sublimation makes one ready to accept substitute gratifications and to become more adaptable to the circumstances of life. She says, "This makes for less accumulated tension, less feeling of frustration, and creates new and important sources of happiness and satisfaction in life."

Some of our most dedicated teachers and priests and social-service workers have turned their love impulses into loving others in rich and meaningful ways. Ghandi and Schweitzer and Jane Addams and Eleanor Roosevelt are but a few of the great souls who found the meaning of love beyond the simple sex act. You are no saint, you say. Yet, in a sense, you too must practice some sexual restraint in order even to find yourself.

You need to develop your tastes and talents before you are ready to give yourself fully to any lover. You grow up best when you do not rush into active sexuality before you have found your own potentialities. The individual who is pushed early into an active sex life finds it more difficult to study and to learn and to travel and to develop than does the youth who diverts some of his sexual energy into other channels for a while.

Dr. Benjamin Spock puts this point well when he says that sexuality is not a simple instinct in human beings at all. In growing up, a great part of one's sexual longing is transmuted into such precious qualities as tenderness, chivalry, altruism, and dreams of marital devotion, home, and children. It is through the subtle transformations of sexuality that the wellsprings of creativity pour forth in the arts, the sciences, and even in the desire to study. If all of your sex drive were immediately released in intercourse, your full potentiality for becoming your own best self would suffer.

Even in marriage there are periods of high creativity when sex activity ceases for a while. During the last part of her pregnancy, and for weeks afterward, a woman does not cohabit with her husband. When a man is pouring himself into his work, or throwing himself into some community project, his intimate moments with his wife may be less frequent for a while. Authors and artists, doctors and politicians spend themselves in their beloved work at times, returning to their spouses with a new sense of fulfillment.

Restraint is part of the price we pay for human development. You restrain your need for sleep in order to get your studying done. You control your desire for food in order to keep in trim and remain in good health. You depart from your instinct of self-preservation in order to be brave and avoid cowardice. You control your acquisitive drives or risk becoming greedy. You develop socially acceptable ways of meeting and living with others in business and social interaction. You restrain your sexual impulses in order to continue to enjoy your freedom among others. You delay your sex experience until you are ready for the responsibilities of building a family. You postpone sexuality now so that you may develop fully as a person as you move toward full adulthood.

The "Try Before You Buy" Fallacy

Are sexual relations the way to know whether two people are compatible? you wonder. The argument is that unless you engage in premarital intercourse, you cannot possibly know whether or not you are sexually suited to one another. You would not buy a pair of shoes without first trying them on, so why take a chance on anything as important as a marriage partner? is the way teen-agers sometimes put the question.

This is the "try before you buy" fallacy. It ignores a number of known facts about sexual adjustment. To begin with, the picturesque analogy of buying shoes breaks down when you realize that a foot stays about the same size, but that the woman's vagina is wonderfully stretchable. It can enlarge to accommodate the birth of a baby, or to fit the male organ of any size comfortably.

It is wise to test your compatibility *as persons*. This involves getting really well acquainted with one another in a wide variety of settings and activities so that you can see how your interests, temperaments, and values match in real life situations. The better you know one another as persons, the better prepared for marriage you are. Establishing your identity as a pair before you get married and live together as man and wife is a good idea.

Statistical evidence that premarital experience is a questionable foundation for successful marriage is not hard to come by. Professors Burgess and Wallin found that engaged couples who had intercourse had lower engagement scores than did those who had none before marriage. They found that marital love was favorably associated with premarital chastity in both sexes. They concluded that chastity was favorable to both one's own marriage adjustment and to that of one's spouse. Dr. Terman found the highest marital happiness among couples who were virgins at marriage. Dr. Harvey Locke's research comparing happily married with divorced couples found a significantly larger percentage of divorced men than happily married ones reporting premarital intercourse. Dr. Kinsey found that women who had responded sexually before marriage made *quicker* sexual adjustments after they married. But this difference between those with and without premarital sex experience narrows through the early years of marriage.

"Neither delayed marriage nor lack of previous sexual experience is a hindrance to a woman's good sexual adjustment," concludes one nationwide study of the question. The American Institute of Family Relations collected confidential data from two thousand married college-level women from every part of the United States. These educated wives responded anonymously to questions about their premarital and marital experience.

At the beginning of their marriage, 28 per cent of the virgins at marriage and 39 per cent of the non-virginal brides were responding sexually to their husbands. In less than a year after marriage, an additional 40 per cent of the virgins at marriage and 22 per cent of the non-virgins had succeeded in achieving a good sexual response if they had not started with it. Eventually, 86 per cent of the premarital virgins and 85 per cent of the non-virgins were sexually responsive. The report concludes that "previous sexual experience of a woman is no help to her in making a good sexual adjustment in her marriage."

Courtship and engagement periods are shorter among those couples who go all the way before marriage. Dr. Eugene Kanin of Purdue University finds that couples go steady and are engaged for a significantly longer time when they wait until marriage. This gives them time to get to know one another as persons, to make plans for their marriage, and to build a sound foundation for their life together, which may be lacking for the couple already having sexual relations. Fear of pregnancy or the pregnancy itself hastens the wedding date for many a couple, before one or both are really ready to settle down. Dr. Kanin mentions such additional factors as anxiety concerning male exploitation and the possible shift to a lover-mistress relationship, fear of discovery, and feelings of guilt, as tending to shorten the insecure courtship period.

Couples who have already begun to have sexual relations before marriage tend to avoid having a honeymoon. Having a honeymoon before settling down "as an old married couple" is important to many people. They feel that they should take marriage seriously, prepare for it well, and get it off to a good start in an honest-to-goodness honeymoon. They may be the romantic ones, who are willing to wait till marriage before attempting to live together as man and wife. They may be the responsible ones who prefer to follow conventional standards.

The conclusion is that premarital testing is not necessarily a good way to start a life together. Some couples may do it and are glad they did. But there are many more successful marriages among those who wait till marriage before going all the way.

Venereal Disease Is Still a Real Danger

Now that venereal infections can be cleared up with a shot or two of penicillin, is there any danger in sexual contacts anymore? Modern young people want to know whether there is anything to the warnings they hear, or whether the warnings of the dangers of sexually contracted disease are based upon outmoded fears.

Not long ago young people were frightened by gruesome stories of what happened to persons with venereal disease. They were told the dreadful details of what havoc such infections could cause in both sexes. They were impressed with how long it would take to be cured once they had contracted one of these diseases. Efforts were made by some adults to make people afraid of venereal disease. But fear alone boomerangs. And venereal diseases are increasingly a problem.

In 1947, in the aftermath of World War II, there were more than one hundred thousand (107,716) cases of infectious syphilis in the United States. By 1953, only 9,551 cases were reported, making social-health leaders wonder whether their active campaigns to eradicate the venereal diseases had definitely licked the problem. But by 1958 the trend of infectious syphilis turned upward, followed in 1960 and 1961 by 50 per cent increases each year. By 1963, after five years of annual increases, there were four and one-half times as many cases as were reported in 1957—an increase of 448 per cent! And the rise in the incidence of syphilis has been much sharper for persons under twenty years of age than for all other age groups combined.

The United States Public Health Service considers infectious syphilis rates the best indicators of the incidence of venereal disease. But gonorrhea is even more prevalent and widespread than syphilis. State health departments continue to report more than twice as many cases of gonorrhea as syphilis. Although they are two different diseases, they both are caught and spread through sexual contact, and so are considered together as venereal diseases.

"Venereal" means related to or associated with sexual contact. Syphilis is an infectious disease caused by a microscopic organism called a spirochete because of its spiral shape. Spirochetes are passed from one body to another in the intimate contact of moist body surfaces, during sexual intercourse. Gonorrhea, caused by gonococcus bacteria, is also caught in sexual intimacies.

Both syphilis and gonorrhea are sneaky diseases. There is no immediate pain when they start. But untreated syphilis is a killer that takes many forms, often after years of dormancy in the diseased individual. Gonorrhea is one cause of sterility in women (by closing the infected tubes). The eyes of babies born to women with gonorrhea may be infected at birth. If untreated, this infection causes blindness. Early syphilis can be detected by blood tests. But gonorrhea can be diagnosed only by smears and cultures.

No vaccines against syphilis or gonorrhea are available. There are no completely effective ways of avoiding infection except to refrain from intercourse with infected persons. How can you know whether an individual is infected? You can't. There are no outward indications by which you can tell who has a venereal disease. Only qualified medical personnel can diagnose these diseases.

How are venereal diseases controlled? Says Dr. Evan Thomas:

Apart from advising against sexual promiscuity, these diseases can only be treated by finding infectious cases and treating them. This means that every infected individual should be interviewed for sexual contacts. The contacts must be found, examined and treated.

Venereal disease can be treated safely only by doctors. Only physicians can tell when their patients are safely cured. There are dangers in trying to treat yourself. You may not cure the disease completely. You can get bad side effects. You can spread the infection to others before you are out of the infectious stage. Teen-agers with venereal disease are not limited to school drop-outs from poor neighborhoods. There are "nice respectable" young people still in school who get and pass on venereal infections. For instance, a highly intelligent and attractive high-school girl had infrequent relations with her steady boy friend. One night they quarreled, and in anger he had sexual relations with a pick-up. He contracted syphilis and passed it along to his sweetheart without either of them knowing what was happening.

Dr. Celia Deschin, who reports this case, has recently completed a study of six hundred teen-agers with venereal disease. She found that nine out of ten young people do not have a very good knowledge of venereal infection. Most of them get their sex education from other teen-agers, who themselves are confused about the real facts. Her findings suggest that too many young people today have a false sense of security about sex. They feel safe because they have heard that venereal diseases are now easy to cure.

The catch is that the problem is not so much medical as social. When a young person comes immediately to a clinic or a doctor after sexual intercourse, he or she can be treated appropriately and completely. But there are reasons why so many do not take this kind of responsibility. They feel ashamed of what they have done. They are afraid that their parents and friends will find out. They hope that they have been lucky this time. They naively suppose that because they know the sex partner, everything will be all right. They do not want to "tell on" their sex partner by reporting the incident. They take a chance, and thereby carry their infection to others. It spreads, and the problem is out of hand again.

Education based upon the facts of the case can help a teen-ager keep his conduct in line with his life plans. Even among young people in venereal-disease clinics, those who acquired their knowledge about sex from home, school, or sex-educational books were far less promiscuous than those whose knowledge came from less reliable sources. Since promiscuous activity is much more likely to expose a person to venereal infection, constructive sex education should help young people avoid infection.

Premarital chastity and postmarital fidelity still remain the best safeguards against the dangers of venereal infection.

Chastity Can Be Worth the Struggle

A wise woman doctor once said that chastity is a battleground in which the stakes are high—so high that they make the struggle worth while. She went on to detail why so many intelligent girls lose this battle for their own highest values. First, is the girl's eagerness to give of herself. She wants to be wanted, and she wants to give. This is a wonderful feeling, but a girl should know what it is that she is giving. There are times when, wanting to give a little, she gives too much. It is hard for a generous-hearted girl to know where and how to stop when the decision must be made.

Secondly, Dr. Hilliard mentions the girl who becomes possessive of her boy friend after she has given herself to him. What such a girl often does not see is that you lose what you want most by insisting upon possessing it. No one can possess the life of another. Love holds with an open hand, never with a tight fist.

Third, the physician discusses the triggering of desire that neither fellow nor girl knows how to curb. An easy friendship traveling at a comfortable thirty miles an hour can shift without warning to a blinding passion racing along at a hundred miles an hour. A glandular whim makes a mockery of conscience and discretion.

An unmarried mother waiting out her pregnancy describes the increasing crescendo of sexual stimulation from her own experience. "I know, to me and to most of the kids I know, it just kind of went a little bit further each time, and finally you aren't a virgin anymore. You start out to do a little petting, and before you realize what is happening, you can't stop. Then, it's not so easy to say "No" next time, or the next time, or the next, and the first thing you know you're pregnant."

Here is part of a recent news story of an unmarried father:

> During these painful months, Kenneth learned, as in no other way, the full, bitter implications of illicit love. From the questions he asked about Joan and the baby, he showed his growing realization of how heavy a price premarital sex can exact. He would repeat: "It's not worth it."
>
> When the baby was born, Kenneth, at his own request, visited the hospital to see his healthy chubby daughter. He stared at her silently for a long time. Then he put his hands up to his face as though he was going to cry. He managed to control himself.
>
> "All those other babies will be going home," he said in a barely audible, shaky voice. "My God, what have I done?"

These young people have learned a hard lesson, that once the heat of sexuality takes over, you no longer have a choice. With your first sex experience, you are no longer a virgin. Whether you feel it is perfectly safe for you or not, you can choose only once to go all the way before marriage. As long as you wait, you still have the freedom to choose when and with whom and under what circumstances you will give yourself to another human being in the most intimate contact possible for you.

7

Is Pregnancy

Is there any reason to fear that you might become a parent before you intend to? You frequently hear the question, Why wait until marriage now that "the pill" has been developed? You, too, may wonder why you should not go as far as you like in your love-making now that contraceptives could protect you from possible pregnancy.

If methods of preventing conception are that good, why is it that so many girls get into trouble? If birth-control procedures are that infallible, why is that so many fellows ask, "My girl is pregnant. Do I have to marry her?" If couples are that sure about not getting caught, why are so many couples afraid of the possibility of an unplanned pregnancy? These are good questions that deserve valid answers. The simple fact is that pregnancy still is a possibility, for a number of reasons.

Why Pregnancy Is Still a Possibility

1. Scientific knowledge is no more effective than the use persons make of it. Research in developing new contraceptives has made great progress. But still, even married couples continue to have babies they have not planned. A study on a midwestern campus of married university students found that two-thirds of their first pregnancies were unplanned. A married public-health nurse not long ago reported that she had had four pregnancies in five years and wanted to avoid another baby at least for a while. She asked for family-planning help, saying, "We've tried everything, but nothing works for us." Americans seem to be more fertile now that most of us are so well fed. Planned parenthood has become more complicated with so many forms and methods of birth control available. At the present writing there are at least six different oral contraceptives on the market, each with its own specific dosage and required regimen. It takes a good deal of responsibility and know-how to make any method completely effective.

2. Most young people are not well-informed about sex and reproduction. Sex education is generally inadequate. Confusion is widespread about even the most basic biological facts of life. Nationwide studies find that less than half of today's teen-agers

A Possibility?

get their sex information from such responsible adults as parents, doctors, or religious leaders.

Adults themselves are often unsure about the sexual side of life. Interviews with more than ten thousand men and women found many a grown man and woman "appallingly, sometimes tragically, ignorant of even simple sex facts after years of marriage." For instance, one out of four of both men and women thought that a woman's chances of becoming pregnant are greatly reduced if she does not respond during intercourse. Actually, the female's sexual response has no effect on her chance of becoming pregnant. One-third of the women and one-half of the men did not know when a woman is most likely to conceive.

The new contraceptives are often misunderstood. One high-school girl "borrowed" one of her mother's pills as she left for a big week end with her boy friend. She did not realize that one pill was completely ineffective as a contraceptive for her, since a series of pills must be taken each month. She therefore had no protection from getting pregnant herself. And by removing one pill from her mother's monthly series, she placed her mother in a situation where she, too, might become pregnant.

3. Romantic ideas sometimes prevent a couple from taking appropriate precautions. Some girls say they do not want to be so practical as to use methods of preventing conception. They think it is somehow nicer just to be carried away on the spur of the moment. One girl, waiting for her baby to be born, told why she had not safeguarded herself from having an illegitimate baby: "It just happened. I did not use anything and I guess he didn't either. It just didn't seem right to be so businesslike about it."

There is an element of fatalism in attitudes toward becoming pregnant that some young people hold. They talk about having "an accident" or "getting caught" or "taking a chance" as though somehow the responsibility for conceiving or not starting a baby were somehow not theirs. Recent research studies find such irresponsibility especially on the part of couples who do not care deeply for one another. A boy is apt to feel more responsible for a girl when he sees her as his wife-to-be. Being responsible as a couple, and planning for all future contingencies, occurs more frequently among real lovers than among less-involved pairs.

4. Because many people believe that using birth-control devices is immoral, dissemination of knowledge about medically approved contraceptives is generally curtailed. Public hospitals do not routinely provide family-limitation advice even to the mothers who request it. In some states the giving of birth-control information is illegal. Schools generally do not include such information in their programs. Churches only occasionally provide instruction about responsible parenthood for their constituents. In many a modern community it is probably harder to find out about controlling fertility than almost any other area of life.

5. Unmarried young people are particularly handicapped in obtaining reliable contraceptives. Doctors, clinics, schools, and colleges generally tend to limit birth-control advice and materials to women who are already married. Most effective methods of planned parenthood require a doctor's prescription—not easy to come by when a girl is not yet married. The devices that are available without a prescription are not completely reliable. Some over-the-counter medications are not safe; many are ineffective. No wonder pregnancy becomes a problem for many a young couple who "go all the way."

When a Girl Gets Pregnant, What Can She Do?

When an unmarried girl becomes pregnant, she has three choices. She can terminate the pregnancy. She can get married to give her child a name. She can have her baby without getting married. None of these alternatives is satisfactory. All have their problems and their pain.

Few people advocate abortions. Yet a million or more take place every year in the United States. Many of these are performed on married women who for one reason or another cannot see their way clear to having another child. The rest are sought as the single girl's answer to the problem of unwelcome pregnancy.

Once a girl or woman decides that she cannot possibly have the child she has conceived, she then faces the question as to how she will go about terminating her pregnancy. She has four possible courses of action, no one of which is pleasant. (1) She can try to terminate her pregnancy herself, only to find that self-induced abortion attempts rarely work, and can be deadly dangerous. (2) She can patronize an "abortion ring" in her area. When she does, she runs the risk of careless procedures with the possibility of infection and neglect. An estimated five thousand girls and women lose their lives every year from unskilled abortions in the United

States. (3) She can go to a doctor who takes a chance that he won't be caught giving her the abortion. Terminating a pregnancy without sufficient medical justification is illegal in the United States; therefore, physicians' fees are high. The operation involves secrecy and speed, but in the hands of a qualified professional person it does not need to be hazardous to the girl's life and health. (4) She can take a trip to a country with more lenient abortion policies and have the pregnancy terminated in a hospital with good medical attention. This is expensive. It takes the girl among strangers speaking another language, with whom she may feel alone and lonely at a difficult period at best.

Terminating a pregnancy is a serious step. Even if the girl has no ill effects physically, she may suffer such psychological after-effects as guilt, shame, worry, nervousness, depression, and fear of exposure, even blackmail. The fact that in the United States abortion is generally considered both morally and legally wrong cannot be ignored.

Many a girl advances her wedding date when she learns that she is pregnant. Professor Christensen's studies indicate that approximately one out of every five first babies in the United States is conceived before the parents marry. Sometimes the young pair have to falsify their ages in order to get a marriage license. If they have been planning to get married all along, they hurry up and make their union legal when they discover they are going to have a baby.

A girl may have to pressure her fellow to "do the right thing." If she is a strong-willed girl, she says, "Look here, boy, we are going to get married or else." She may weep or plead with a reluctant lover in order to make official the relationship that is about to make them parents. A boy not ready for marriage and fatherhood may panic and run. He may disclaim his responsibility by suggesting that if the girl would go all the way with him, she might with any man, and that he may not be the father of the baby. He, as well as the girl, may feel trapped. The "have-to" marriage starts under a shadow touched as often as not with deceit, disappointment, and disapproval on the part of the pair, their friends, and families.

One unhappy mother told of her son and his girl coming home when they were both juniors in high school to announce, "Well, we have to get married." The parents said, "If you have to, you have to," only reluctantly giving their permission. Before the young wife was twenty, she had three babies, a dirty house, and a husband who got out as often as he could. She went to work not only for the money, but to get away from the children. Then she began having affairs with the milkman, a next-door neighbor, and the precinct captain before her young husband got fed up and left. An unhappy story without a happy ending for the young pair, their children, or the grandparents who are trying to help.

Occasionally one hears of a pregnant girl who accepts as a husband any available man or boy who will give her baby a name. It usually is not the kind of marriage the girl had in mind, but it appears to look better than having an illegitimate baby. This kind of union sometimes works out eventually, especially if the man is able to love his wife and her child. But it takes the girl a while to get over the feeling of being damaged goods, "picked up on the bargain counter," as one unhappy teen-ager put it.

The third course open to the pregnant girl is to go ahead and have her baby without getting married. Currently there are some 250,000 illegitimate births a year in this country. In a society in which having a baby out of wedlock is a disgrace, how does a girl go about having her baby and still save face?

The usually recommended procedure is for the girl to go to a home for unmarried mothers in a large city, where she can have her baby safely and in relative secrecy. She is assured of good pre-natal and delivery care not so easy in other settings. She can have her baby and place it for adoption, to be brought up by a family ready to give it a good home.

Some families send a pregnant daughter to visit some distant relative until after the baby comes. In order to cover up their shame, they announce that the girl is going away to school or to help care for some aging or infirm family member for the rest of the year. This effort at deceit and pretense is only partially suc-cessful in most cases. It is a dubious "solution" dependent upon burdening another family with a problem too hot to handle at home.

One knows of an occasional older girl who gets an apartment, and when her time comes, delivers her child under an assumed name in a nearby hospital. She finds herself in the maternity wing without the beaming husband, the proud parents, and the thought-ful gifts that make having a baby so wonderful within marriage.

When a girl gets pregnant, she is wise to consult a responsible adult as soon as possible. Telling her mother may not be easy, but it may be the best thing to do in the long run. Talking over her problem with her doctor and possibly with her pastor may be of considerable help. Somehow, she must face the real alternatives she has, and work out with the adults who care for her the plan that seems most feasible.

What Can an Unmarried Girl Do with Her Baby?

Pregnancy ends in childbirth with the inevitable question of who will rear the baby. If the parents are married, they expect of course to bring up and love and care for their children. But when an unmarried mother brings her child into the world, she is faced with the heavy responsibility of deciding what to do with her little foundling. With her child's future in mind, a girl may choose to place her baby in adoption. She probably will never know who has her baby or how he is faring. But she can be sure that the adoptive agency will choose a family that will give her baby a good home through the years. Some babies are easier to place than are others. Between 1940 and 1958 most illegitimate white babies (70 per cent) were adopted, but only 5 per cent of the Negro babies were adopted in the United States. Babies of mixed parentage are especially hard to find homes for in most countries.

A desperate girl may abandon her baby. A recent news story told of a young mother walking out of Cook County Hospital, leaving her baby behind. When the officials found the mother the next day, she told them that she did not want the baby and did not care what the hospital did with it. The baby was put in the "boarder baby" ward in the county's children's hospital, where there were already more than eighty such abandoned babies. This resembles the leaving-the-baby-on-the-doorstep that unmarried mothers traditionally practiced. It is better by far than the ash can method, in which the mother literally destroys her newborn infant. In a large state university such a case turned up not long ago. A co-ed braved through her pregnancy, gave birth to her baby in the girls' domitory, and then quietly disposed of it without rousing her roommates.

You possibly have known of one or more cases in which the girl gave her baby to her mother to rear while she went back to school. In some neighborhoods this is not uncommon. One mother we know is bringing up her daughter's child along with her own youngest, born the same month. For the curious, the two babies are passed off as twins. They bear the same name, and actually look very much alike. Right now the daughter is in love with a man who wants to marry her, and she is trying to decide whether to tell him the truth in order to make a home for her baby, or not to risk losing him by confessing that her "sister" is in truth her own baby. It is not an easy decision. There are no easy ways out of unwed motherhood.

The final course open to the unmarried mother is to try to rear her child herself, alone. This is a heavy responsibility anywhere. In Denmark there are government homes for unwed mothers and their babies. The children are cared for while their mothers work through the day. The mothers have each other for company, they sometimes entertain, and attempt to live as normally as they can without husbands. Without official support, this solution is an especially burdensome one. The young mother must work in order to support her child and herself. Baby-sitters are hard to come by in most places. At an age when a girl normally is out having good times with other fellows and girls, the unmarried mother is home alone with her baby night after night. One is forced to the conclusion that having a baby without a home in which to bring it up poses serious problems—for the girl, her family, the boy friend, and for the baby.

The Price You Pay, as a Girl, as a Boy

Start a baby before you get married, and you pay a heavy price. The chances are the girl will have to drop out of school. With little education and no job training her outlook for the future is poor. The boy, too, faces a threat to his educational and vocational plans, as many an unmarried father recognizes.

Such a case is reported in a recent issue of *Children* (March–April, 1963):

> Robert said he had engaged in sexual relations with Barbara because his friends were having sexual experiences, and he could not see anything wrong with this and no reason why he should not. Although he and Barbara had had such relations over a period of time, the experiences had been unsatisfactory for him and left him feeling depressed. After his first sexual experience, he felt so badly he went to his church to seek the youth counselor in order to talk with him about his feelings. The youth counselor was not available and Robert did not pursue this further. He had known about contraceptives and had made some efforts to use them, but had abandoned their use because he did not like the idea, and so took no precautions to prevent pregnancy.
>
> Robert said he had never entertained the idea of marriage during his relationship with Barbara. When he learned that she

was pregnant, he had thought briefly of this possibility and quickly dismissed it. He said he was not ready for marriage nor did he feel that if he were that he would want to marry Barbara. His plans were to finish high school and go into the Navy where he could attend a technical school . . .

Both the fellow and the girl can find their social life limited once they get involved sexually. A college housemother says that she sees a considerable amount of self-righteousness among her girls when a co-ed gets pregnant. Some of the students rally around and may try to help out their troubled classmate. But if she gives the impression that she has done nothing wrong, they drop her like a hot potato. The impression is that a girl who gets into trouble should be contrite and truly sorry for what she has done in order to get any sympathy from others. Most communities expect that once students get in the family way, they will drop out of the regular social activities of the school. Now that they are married, or going to have a baby, the reasoning goes, they have withdrawn themselves from usual teen-age social life.

The "shotgun" or the hurried-up marriage is usually a poor solution to the problem of pregnancy. The girl and the boy quite likely feel rushed into domestic responsibilities before they are ready to settle down. They feel tied down, trapped, and cornered by their predicament. This may be one reason why "have-to" marriages so often end in divorce, as Dr. Christensen's studies have found to be the case.

Even when the educational, vocational, and marital problems are not too great, the mental torment of premarital pregnancy can be real. According to Professor Kirkendall, most sexually experienced young people find their interpersonal relationships disappointing. Dr. Vincent reports that some of the unmarried mothers he studied had reactions of disgust and disillusionment. One sixteen-year old pregnant girl told him,

Everything you read in books about love is a bunch of lies. It isn't tender; it isn't sweet and enduring. It is cruel and it hurts. Movie writers in this country ought to be jailed for writing all that junk about moonlight and roses. What's more all those fade-outs they do in the movies and stories when people are supposed to be loving and everything is so romantic and the next morning everyone is so happy . . . it isn't like that at all. It hurts; it hurts terribly when you are not used to it. Moreover you feel awful the next day when your boyfriend won't even look at you.

Or, here is the way a college freshman reacted to her pregnancy:

> What does a 19-year old female like me want with a baby? I had all I wanted of them with my three kid brothers and sisters. What a way to start a college career. Even if no one back home finds out about it, I will have a sweet time talking my way back into school after leaving in the middle of the semester. I have never felt worse in my life . . . mentally or physically . . . and each day gets worse. . . .

The he-done-her-wrong theme is not hard to find in actual girls' experiences. One puts her disillusionment this way:

> No one could feel as degraded and short-changed as I. He promised all sorts of things; he came through with nothing. I would never have gone an inch of the way with him if I even suspected that the minute I got pregnant he would run out. Now I hold the bag; he goes merrily on his way probably doing the same thing all over again with others. I was really taken in, and he was a lousy lover to boot.

Granted that unmarried girls and fellows sometimes feel some of the positive fulfillment that comes from producing a new human being, but their oft-reported negative reactions are real and tragic. One sixteen-year-old girl, writing to a consultant at the Children's Bureau, put the dilemma of many a pregnant schoolgirl into the following words:

> I am 16 years old and expecting a baby in 4 months. I am the only one who knows about this. Although I am practically starving myself to death I fear that it will become noticeable and I cannot get away with this much longer. My mother and father will kill me if they know about this and that is why I must get away from here.
>
> I have another reason too for being unable to stay at home. I am sure you are aware of just how miserable a girl can be among gossips. I just must finish high school next year and if this gets around I will never be able to face my friends and classmates again.
>
> For so long now I have cried myself out and now I have decided to keep a cool head and do the best I can. I want to go away on the pretext of visiting friends. I could use their address when I write home . . . However, I have no money to pay a doctor or hospital. Is there a place where I could go and get a job—perhaps in a hospital so I could work for my expenses?

. . . Thank you for letting me tell you my troubles. You are the one and only person who shares my secret and it feels good to have told someone. It has been a great mental strain and quite difficult to keep up a good front to hide my true anxieties. A secret like this is very hard to live with alone.

In spite of all the freedom modern young people enjoy, there are still harsh penalties for the couple who step out of line. The pregnant unmarried girl is still disapproved of by adults, pitied by her classmates, asked to leave school, and/or drop out of normal social activities, and is often sent packing to have her baby among strangers. The boy who gets a girl into trouble is often known in today's communities where everyone knows who is going with whom. Whether he marries the girl or not, he lives under the shadow of their mutual mistake. His social and vocational opportunities are often curtailed, and he either brazens it out or leaves town to make a new start somewhere else. The hurried-up marriage may appear to be the way out, but in actual practice can be a tragic disappointment.

Going all the way without getting pregnant is possible in theory, but is difficult in actual practice. Pregnancy is always a possibility as the natural outcome of sexual intercourse. The story of creation can be re-enacted whenever male and female mate. The only protection is to be responsible for the consequences of one's behavior.

As the official handbook on sex instruction published by the Royal Board of Education in Sweden concludes,

> Love between a man and a woman . . . *is not only their private affair,* even though it may at a superficial glance appear so. For it is a concern of the whole *community* that the children they produce should be given good care and upbringing. Marriage is the form of living together by which the community is best able to ensure security and care for the rising generation. . . .
>
> Sexual intercourse must therefore always take place with a feeling of *responsibility* and with *regard to the consequences.* This attitude to intercourse in which consideration is given to the good of the children means living a life of continence during adolescence and until one is in a position to set up a home.

Is anything less advisable in the United States? Now, when so many arguments for permissiveness flourish among young and not-so-young people, it is time for all of us to clarify our sex standards.

8   *Would You Like To*

Who has not dreamed of what it would be like to live without restraints? Men and women of all ages have pictured the delights of a carefree existence where living is easy and sex is simple. Stories of life on an island in the South Seas abound. You can hear the surf pounding upon the sun-drenched beach. The palms wave lazily overhead. Food drops freely from the trees, or swims into the fishing net. Thatched huts and woven mats solve the housing problem. Flashing smiles, simple clothes, and readily accessible partners under the moon take care of the sex drive. What else could one want? Where is the shadow in such a picture?

For the past several decades, anthropologists have been providing accurate accounts of life in the more permissive societies around the world. Sociologists have been making comparative studies of various cultures in which sex is differently viewed. Psychologists and psychiatrists have been reporting how men and women feel in different social situations. Therefore, permissiveness is no longer just a pleasant daydream, but a condition that can be understood and evaluated.

The Effect of Permissiveness on the Relationship

Tenderness tends to lose its importance when sex partners are readily accessible. The male takes the female with a minimum of considerate love-making. Sex is often aggressive and in the nature of an assault in situations where it is easy. Uninhibited intercourse involves little more than a biological release for the fellow, and even less for the girl.

Sex is impersonal when it is unrestrained. When sexual intercourse is not limited to a life partner, the simplest practice is to turn to the nearest sex object. The more readily available sexual activity is, the less emotion there is associated with it. Dr. Ira Reiss compares permissiveness in groups of adults and students in the United States. He finds that the more permissive devalue kissing and petting and give more relative support to intercourse. Remember the girl in Chapter 5 who felt let down because her premarital love affair had become so casual? Instead of the love-making she had enjoyed, she said, "It is all over before I am ready to start. It is getting so I would give up anything just to sit on the sofa and talk and neck a little."

Live Where Sex Is Easy?

Appreciation of the lover as a person is lessened when sex is too quickly a possible connection between them. The most obvious example of this is the lack of appreciation a man has for the prostitute, or she for him. Companionship as two human beings who get to know one another well and enjoy each other as individuals is difficult to establish without the time and sexual restraint required to build a complete relationship.

Fidelity is not valued in a culture that allows sexual contact with any ready mate at any time. The kind of permanence that is expected in the mutual pledge of "until death do us part" makes less sense in a permissive culture where sex is sought for sex's sake so long as physical desire lasts. Why be faithful to one when so many other appealing possibilities are available? is the question that has only one clear answer under permissiveness.

Idealization of the loved one is sacrificed in a permissive society. The eminent anthropologist Bronislaw Malinowski tells of the Trobriand Islander for whom sexual access is easy. With no barriers between the sexes, nothing is hidden, and very little is left to the imagination. When sexual needs are immediately and easily satisfied, there is no need for dreaming of one's beloved.

Romance is important to Americans. Companionship is what both men and women look forward to in marriage. Companionship means tenderness, concern for the other as a person while being understood and encouraged as a personality oneself. Companionship involves appreciation and fidelity, some idealization and romance—to most of us. These ingredients of companionship are threatened by sexual permissiveness before marriage. You may want to think twice before you sacrifice the possibility of lifelong companionship for a policy of permissiveness, either before or after you are married.

What Does a Girl Have to Lose?

A girl has nothing to lose but her virginity, according to the freedom school of sex. Actually, she has a great deal more at stake. In a permissive culture, a girl becomes easy prey to any male strong enough to take her. She is introduced to sexual activity by older men and boys before she herself is ready or interested.

Unless she is protected and taught to protect herself, she becomes an easy mark for any designing male. This is true not only in the simple societies where sex is generally encouraged; it holds for girls and women within any culture who are available to men with a permissive or exploitative outlook.

The attractive girl is exploited sexually by men who seek sex partners without restraint. She may long to feel that she is loved as a woman, but soon discovers that it is her build rather than she herself that is admired. She finds it hard to feel that she is desirable as an individual when men seek her only for the sexual satisfaction they find in her body. The tragic life histories of many of our most attractive women are mute evidence of the difficulty the beautiful girl has in establishing herself as a person in her relationships with men.

The less desirable girl in a permissive culture may fare badly for quite another reason. Because men leave her alone for more-attractive females, she may be an easy mark for the love-em-and-leave-em fellow. When she feels threatened by her lack of masculine attention, she may throw herself away in some tawdry episode that gives her little of the sense of being loved, and only compounds her feeling of unworthiness. Many a fellow exploits the ugly duckling of a girl, makes a slave of her, dumps his homework on her desk, and capitalizes on her lack of sex appeal by having her do his chores.

Youth is sexually desirable. In a permissive culture, it is the young maiden who attracts the men and boys. Since there is always a new crop of young girls coming along, this puts the older girls and women in a situation of decreasing popularity. The older a woman is, the more important security in affection becomes to her. Yet this is assured only by sexual restraint and fidelity. One of the simple facts of life is that one thing every girl is sure to lose is her youth. Building a strong permanent relationship with a man through the years is the best safeguard a girl has for her life as a woman, a beloved sex partner, a wife, and a mother. This is a strong argument for premarital fidelity that many a modern girl would do well to learn.

C. S. Lewis, eminent English author, says that present-day signs of women's desperate competition for men's attention fills him with pity. He points to the disadvantage women face in the ruthless war of promiscuity. They play for higher stakes than men do and are more likely to lose, for the simple reason that their physical beauty decreases every year after they become mature.

They spend hundreds of millions of dollars on cosmetics with which to attract and hold their men. But the charm of maturity is in the personality. Feminine appeal through mind and spirit as well as sexuality is permanently possible.

What Does a Fellow Have to Lose?

Permissiveness generally favors the man. It gives him the freedom to move from female to female without the responsibility of monogamy or fidelity. It allows him sexual release from the time he matures without undue restraint. It provides him with access to any girl or woman whom he can woo to his way of thinking at any time, without marriage or commitment. With all this, what has a fellow to lose? A boy risks the competition of older, stronger, more attractive men for the most desirable females. Since boys mature later than girls in general, this means that by the time a boy is ready to play house in a sexual sense, the girls of his age or a little younger have already been taken by the more mature fellows. He therefore will have to fight for the girl's attention, or be satisfied with the females that have been tossed aside by their previous partners.

In a permissive culture, a fellow cannot be sure that his girl will wait for him when he leaves for a while. As his work and other interests take him away from time to time, he cannot be completely sure that his woman will be faithful while he is gone. There have to be sexual restraints and controls within both the society and the persons to give either men or women a sense of security with their mates.

If a relationship can be broken off at any time, the fellow risks the ongoing companionship with his girl in any deep and permanent sense. When sex liaisons can be made or ended at will, a man loses the chance to become intimately related to his partner as a companion. He does not as fully understand her, nor can she as completely identify herself with him as is possible in a permanent partnership. If all a fellow wants is sexual release, permissiveness is promising. But the boy or man who wants a personal relationship with depth and continuity with his sweetheart, finds all this incompatible with sexual freedom.

A male's only assurance of fatherhood is his faith in fidelity. A man who is not sure of his woman can never be completely sure that her children are his. This doubt can tear a young fellow apart. The girl he has been going with is pregnant and is urging marriage. He wants to do the right thing, but is not sure that the unborn baby is his. How can he be sure, if the premises they have been operating under are mutually permissive? Even when he gets married, what assurance has he that their children are his, unless he trusts his wife?

Ralph Linton tells of a society in which men are not really a part of family life at all. The woman marries, according to Hindu law, but the marriage is to a stranger and ends in divorce three days later. The husband does not enter the home again. The woman has a series of informal love affairs that establish no permanent bond between the father and his children. If the lovers get along well, their relationship can last for years, but it can be broken without notice. The woman is in complete control of the situation and can dismiss her lover by returning his last gift at any time. She is free to take on several lovers at a time, as is the man. The real family consists of the woman and her sons and daughters. The man as husband and father is an outsider to his own family.

Permissiveness can cost a fellow plenty. He risks not having a loving and faithful wife. He risks losing out as a husband and as a father. He loses the security of being sure that his children are his, and the satisfaction of seeing them grow up through the years. He forfeits his place in the family, as many a "migrating male" does in our own culture. This is a big price to pay for sexual freedom. It is one reason why morality makes sense for men as well as for women.

It Is the Innocents Who Suffer

In a South Sea island village all the children are cared for by any available woman. Nursing mothers offer the nipple to any hungry baby. The women collectively look out for all the village children, regardless of who gave them birth. In such a society an unwed mother is fairly sure that her child will get as good attention as any other youngster. In few other cultures around the world can she be so sure.

In Scandinavia there are government apartments set aside for unmarried mothers and their babies. There the mother gets vocational training while her baby is cared for with the other illegitimate children in the center. But even with such official help, many a girl resorts to abortion when she finds herself pregnant without a husband. Dr. Henrik Hoffmeyer of the Copenhagen Mothers' Aid program reports ten thousand abortion applications, and fifteen thousand illegal abortions in Denmark in a year when some seventy-five thousand births were recorded. Even in a country that views premarital sexual activity more casually than we do, this psychiatrist finds abortion a symptom of the desperate plight of the unwed mother. Her anxiety, panic, and ambivalence drive her to rid herself of her baby even though there are other alternatives.

Early in 1964, Dr. Hoffmeyer beamed a television series to Danish teen-agers on sex, concluding, according to an Associated Press report, "Above all, do only what you think is right. Don't try to act older than you are. Don't feel obligated to do something just because others may be doing it."

Professor Harold Christensen compared Danish sex practices with those in the United States. He found that many more Danish than American young people approved of and practiced premarital intercourse. The percentage of illegitimate babies is more than three times higher in Denmark than it is in Indiana, and more than ten times the percentage of illegitimacy in Utah. He finds further, that distinct majorities of American students prefer to marry virgins, not so highly valued in Scandinavia.

Sex instruction is compulsory in Swedish schools. The *Handbook on Sex Instruction in Swedish Schools* prepared by the Royal Board of Education in Sweden clearly states that a pregnant student not ready to take responsibility for any children who may be born should be removed from school as soon as possible. When she wants to resume her education, it advises her attending some other school, preferably in another district, "because of the attention the case may have aroused locally."

One of the rights of children is to be born into a family that is prepared to care for them through the years. Among many animals the young are cared for by the mother alone. But the human baby needs a father as well as a mother to grow up satisfactorily. As Dr. Ralph Linton, the anthropologist, says, "A woman can conceivably provide for the physical needs of her children without male assistance, but she cannot train her sons in the special male attitudes and activities necessary for their success as men."

Is there any worse feeling that a person can have than to feel that he doesn't belong to anyone? Your author saw such a child in travels in a tropical island recently. Guests were having tea in a gracious home one afternoon when one of the women of the household noted a ragged little boy in the yard. Another member of the family observed that the child had been under the banana tree for several days. So they sent to find out whose child he was. The reply came back, "He says he is nobody's child."

Social Problems Under Permissiveness

When sex is easy, there are social problems that are hard to solve. How to avoid bringing into the world babies whom no one wants is a distasteful, awful challenge in many countries today. Contraception is controversial; even when it is used, it is no cure-all. An enlightened country, Japan, has more abortions than births. In 1962, according to a United Press International report, there were 2,000,000 abortions and 1,600,000 babies born in Japan. Most of these abortions are illegal—with all that means in problems of mental and medical, as well as social and family, problems.

Venereal-disease rates reflect increasing permissiveness among youth both here and in other countries. Sweden's gonorrhea rate has jumped 75 per cent in five years, and of last year's new cases, 52 per cent were teen-agers, according to the March 6, 1964, report in *Time*. The best control for venereal infection is premarital chastity and postmarital fidelity—a simple health axiom.

Suicide rates are high among these people with permissive relations between men and women. This holds for students here and for countries such as Denmark and Sweden, which have more suicides than can be comfortably explained. A recent four-year study, *Suicide and Scandinavia,* notes differences in relationships between the sexes, methods of family discipline, and general emotionality as being among the factors that appear to be associated with disproportionally large numbers of suicides.

Sexual permissiveness and family instability go together. The highest divorce rates in the United States are in the social groups with the most permissive attitudes toward sex. Professor Christensen found premarital pregnancy associated with divorce in the United States, and in Denmark as well. In study after study, the evidence is clear—it takes responsible people to build good families.

Take the problem into a larger context and ask yourself why the most permissive societies of the South Seas are the more under-developed parts of the world. Where living is easy and sex is simple, there is no reason for striving and learning and growing, either as individuals or as a culture. Our land, in contrast, was built by hard-working, vigorous people who developed a great country, pushed the frontiers from sea to sea, and gave you and me a respect for effort and achievement.

Now that life is easier for us, we run the risk of losing ground in our development if we just "live it up." We can see our present-day frontiers as social ones in which we face a wilderness of unfinished human business. Our choice is to relax and enjoy the

freedom that is ours without thought for tomorrow, or to live up to our potentials responsibly—both as persons and as a nation.

As Dr. Povl W. Toussieng, Danish psychiatrist at the Menninger Clinic, puts it:

> The history of mankind is man's struggle against his impulses. He has never completely won that struggle and there are many defeats, but we cease to be human if we merely give in to our impulses. On that basis, speaking only as a psychiatrist, I would say to youngsters about premarital intercourse: "You shouldn't."

Sex is a part of life. It can be treated in the same way you treat your other impulses—with restraint and respect as a part of your heritage as a human being. You cannot isolate your sex life. It is a part of you and a part of your culture. You cannot have permissiveness in sex standards and some of the other values that you cherish. Your life is a total package.

9   *Religion—How*

You know, darling, that we will have to be very careful when I get back next September, so that we may keep what we would like to save until we get married. Three of us fellows are engaged and two are dating regularly. We got into the subject of premarital intercourse last night, which was very enlightening and reassuring to me. You see, one of the fellows had had intercourse with an ex-girl friend to whom he was once engaged. We found that he was sorry about the experience and felt that intercourse was the direct cause of his breaking up with the girl. It seemed impossible to back up after it had happened and it was either "get married" or "break off."

Another reason for wanting to abstain from premarital relations is my own. If practiced before marriage, sex relations will have no special meaning, and the marriage ceremony will only legalize future intercourse. I want our marriage to be not just a ceremony of civil law, but one blessed by God as Christ Jesus blessed the wedding of Cana. It isn't law that prevents me from asking for or engaging in intercourse. It is love and respect for you and the belief that a greater harmony for both of us will come when we restrict our sex relations to each other—after we marry. I honestly think that the anticipation of the complete expression of love can be enjoyed almost as much as the act itself . . .

Good night, darling. I will never love anyone more except *OUR* God.

This excerpt from a love letter illustrates the kind of purposely chosen restraint that many a religious young person employs to maintain his sex standards. This young fellow is not alone in his convictions by any means. The famous Kinsey studies were not based upon Sunday School premises. Yet they found that of all the factors accounting for premarital sexual restraint, moral objections led the list by a wide margin. Less than half the girls and women mentioned such factors as fear of pregnancy, fear of public opinion, or sexual unresponsiveness as reasons for premarital chastity, while 89 per cent gave moral objections as the basis for abstaining from premarital intercourse. Dr. Kinsey and his col-

Important Is It?

leagues found less premarital coitus among religious men and women of all faiths. These religious individuals felt that premarital sex experience was wrong, and they tended to prefer to wait for marriage before going all the way.

Professors Burgess and Wallin likewise found a straight-line relationship between religious activities and chastity before marriage in the engaged couples they studied. The more often the couple went to church, the less likely they were to have had intercourse. When both the man and his fiancée attended church once a month or more, they tended to be virgins—62.2 per cent. When neither attended church regularly, some 46 per cent had never engaged in intercourse. Of all the couples, those of mixed religions were more apt to be having premarital intercourse than were the couples who belonged to the same religious faith. When the investigators asked for the reasons why these engaged men and women were refraining from premarital intercourse, the most frequent response was that they did not think it was right. More than two-thirds of the men (68.2 per cent) and 86.8 per cent of the women said that they abstained from intercourse because they personally did not consider it to be right. Many of these men (60.6 per cent) and women (40.1 per cent) said they were not having intercourse with their engagement partner because their partner did not consider it right.

Interestingly, both the men and the women underestimated their partner's standards of premarital abstinence. Of the 86.8 per cent of the women who considered sexual relations before marriage to be wrong, only 60.6 per cent of their fiancés mentioned their sweethearts' moral standards as the reason for not going all the way. Of the 68.2 per cent of the men who did not consider premarital sex relations to be right, only 40.1 per cent of their fiancées gave this as their reason for not indulging before marriage.

Studies agree that religious boys and girls, men and women tend to believe they should wait until marriage before having sexual relations.

Conscience as Your Guide

You carry your moral code within you. You have built it up through the years of your development in your family and among your friends. Out of all that you have learned is good or bad, right or wrong, you have fashioned a set of limits for yourself that is known as your conscience.

Your conscience lets you depart only slightly from appropriate conduct before it pulls you up short with its "still, small voice" within you. You feel a nagging sense of unworthiness when you behave in ways that deep within yourself you do not approve. Or you halt yourself at the brink of temptation with the realization, "My conscience won't let me do it."

Dr. O. Hobart Mowrer's work suggests that these built-in restraints are absolutely necessary, not only for the well-being of society, but for the emotional stability of the individual himself. He feels that it is the sense of sin and guilt that plunges us into the kind of emotional illness that is our own personal "hell on earth."

Conscience is more than built-in brakes. In its positive aspects it becomes the steering wheel of your personality. It guides you safely down the road that leads to the kind of life you want to have. It frees you to become your own true self by setting boundaries for free-wheeling conduct. Within the limits of acceptable bounds, you become free to express yourself, and to become the person you envisage yourself to be.

Conscience allows you to move freely among others, accepted and acceptable because you can be trusted. The unrestrained child spontaneously acting out his impulses is forcibly kept within bounds by his parents. They keep him in his play pen, or remove him bodily from danger with a quick "No-No." Only when he learns to control himself, is he free from their constant supervision. So it is as you mature. When you are ready to assume responbility for your own behavior, you are free to live your own life without too many externally imposed restrictions. Your guidelines are within yourself—in the form of your conscience.

The famous Dr. Benjamin Spock develops this point clearly when he says:

> Most young people who have been brought up in families with high ideals will not let themselves get to the point of intercourse until marriage, not because of lack of desire, not because they are timid, but because the girl, knowing herself, knows that she would lose some of her respect for herself. And the boy loves her too much to be willing to hurt her or his ideal of himself.

Positive Satisfaction in Standards

It is possible to find a comfortable sense of security in one's moral standards. Some very young people rebel from what they feel are unwarranted restrictions. More mature individuals find satisfaction in maintaining those standards that make sense. The difference lies in emphasizing ideals rather than prohibitions. Religion helps one prefer to maintain a standard of chastity both for oneself and for those with whom one has intimate contact.

Take Bryce, for instance. He says simply:

> I value virginity both for myself and for the girl I go out with. I think that it is something to be proud of to come to marriage pure and clean from the inside out. I think a girl ought to be glad she saved herself for marriage when she knows and her husband knows without question that he is the only man who has possessed her.

Patricia sees her sex life as a part of her wholehearted loving of her husband. She realizes that the simple release of sexual tension is not love at all. In order for sexual intercourse to have meaning, it must express all three dimensions of love, as the Greeks knew them. One, *agape,* the outpouring of love with no expectation of return. Two, *philia,* knowing the other, understanding, being, and feeling very near another. Three, *eros,* the love that is possessive and longs to be reciprocated. It takes all three to make a woman feel really loved, desirable and desired. And only in marriage can man and woman combine all three in constantly renewing and reassuring ways. This is worth waiting for, worth working toward, worth standing for as a way of life.

Goodness consists not in moral perfection, nor in being "holier than thou." The religious individual tries, sometimes successfully and sometimes incompletely, to live up to his moral standards. He believes that there are rules to the game of life that stem from the nature of reality itself. He calls these eternal verities the will of God. He finds a deeply meaningful satisfaction in attempting to live up to the highest and best that he knows. His faith rests upon his belief that as a child of God, he has a future worth striving toward, so long as he lives.

Most People Want Limits

In sports, everyone recognizes that a player must obey the rules. The fellow who cheats is put out of the game. As Jackie Robinson put it years ago, "A man must show moral restraint to win honors in the world of sport. The athlete who fails at self-policing automatically and foolishly eliminates himself from championship company."

In the business world, transactions are made according to definite regulations. Hundreds of millions of dollars change hands in the stock market simply and quickly because men trust each other. If it were not for the rules that everyone obeyed, there would be financial chaos.

In marriage and family life, mutual faithfulness is expected. The wife who cheats on her husband and the man who steps out on his wife are operating outside the rules, and they know it. The security and satisfaction of family life depend upon mutual trust and respect.

There was a time when rules for premarital behavior were clear. Older people will tell you that when they grew up, there was no question about premarital chastity. Intercourse belonged in marriage, and only in marriage, and that was it. Of course, some overstepped the rules, but they and everyone else knew that what they had done was wrong. Then a young man who struggled with temptation and won was proud of his strength of character. He felt backed up by his home and his church, his friends, and his sense of what was right.

Youth today is often confused about just what is expected. Boys and girls are afraid of being called "square" or "chicken" if they appear to be "too good." The recurring emphasis on the importance of "having fun" sometimes makes stepping out of bounds seem like the thing to do. As one man put it, "a temptation resisted is a temptation wasted" today. Such pressures are in direct opposition to religious emphases on premarital chastity. The result for many a young person is great personal conflict.

Religious conflict over sexual activities is widespread. Dr. Celia Deschin's study of teen-agers who had contracted venereal disease found them not too comfortable about their sexual activities. Some 30 per cent had real religious conflicts about what they had done. Another 40 per cent felt ashamed and dissatisfied with their sex experience. Even among lower-income minority-group teen-agers some seven out of ten are uneasy about disobeying the moral rules they recognize as right.

Young people of both sexes say they would like more definite limits than they now have. Dr. Richard Klemer found 67 per cent of the men and 80 per cent of the women university students he studied saying they would welcome more definite limits on their sexual behavior. More than three-fourths of all these students felt that young people generally want clearer boundaries set by parents and teachers. As one college woman expressed it:

I believe it is certainly true that young people would welcome more definite limits on their moral behavior. Of course the teen-ager will object to these limitations because his peer group expects him to gripe about parental limitations. But actually these limitations give him a sense of security, for then the teen-ager knows what is expected of him.

Dr. Irene Josselyn says that a normal adolescent does not rebel against standards that are basic within the culture.

Those standards are a source of primary security for him as he struggles to pass from childhood to adulthood. What he does rebel against are those aspects of the parent-child relationship that bind him to childhood, even though these aspects may no longer be considered important by the parents.

Today's high school and college students are searching for moral standards. They are raising honest questions about all kinds of personal and social behavior. They look forward to marriage with an eager intensity that flows over into their dating behavior. They dream of companionship and meaningful communication with others. They recognize the virtue of fidelity both before and after marriage. They are looking for limits within which they may function. The chaplain of Columbia University reports that religion in a new sense is growing rapidly in American colleges. He describes this new religion in part as "a personal quest by young men and women for some reasonable guidelines for their own actions."

Respect for Personality

Respect for personality is a central religious teaching. As religious persons we try to relate to each other without invading the integrity or diminishing the dignity of either personality. All of us want to be loved and trusted and respected as persons. We recoil from being exploited for someone else's purposes. As religious individuals we do not use others for our pleasure. The Christian commitment is to treat persons as persons, and to act toward them redemptively.

Dr. Martin Buber, twentieth-century Jewish sage, sees man's relationship to his world as twofold: the I-Thou and I-It relationship. Each involves a different kind of knowledge and a different kind of response. In the I-It relationship one looks upon the other person as a thing, an It, to be used for one's own ends. The other person becomes an object that is consumed, as one would an orange, to satisfy immediate thirsts and hungers. In the I-Thou relationship the other individual is a person in his own right, with interests and integrity and a personality that are cherished. The moment you treat another person as a thing, he becomes an It rather than a Child of God in his relationship with you. You do wrong when you love things and use persons. You are morally right as you use things and love persons.

As the chaplain of Mt. Holyoke College expresses it,

> Each of us knows that the only kind of life that will ever make sense is one in which the I-Thou relationship is supreme. For this is the kind of love that is patient and kind and not arrogant or rude. It does not insist on its own way; it is not irritable or resentful; it does not rejoice at wrong, but rejoices in the right. It bears all things. So faith, hope, love abide, these three, but the greatest of these is love.

The ethically religious person is concerned for the growth of personality in other persons as well as in himself. Professor Blaine M. Porter puts the point this way:

> The conduct of one's sex life should be focused on how it contributes to helping an individual become a person—a more complete person. Judgment and decision must be based on sound principles of human growth and development and not on the pleasure principle. This conduct should be such that it will contribute to growth, increase maturity, respect for self and others, and the well being of everyone involved. An ethical orientation is a concern for what one's actions will mean and do to others; it poses the question whether what one does or expects will be injurious, humiliating, or otherwise damaging to the other person's integrity and dignity, and will be damaging or undesirable to one's self as a personality. An ethical action, therefore, is one that rejects the use of another person as an instrument or object to be used or coerced for any purpose, no matter how socially or personally desirable that purpose may seem.

The simple fact is that you become what you are to be in interaction with others. You find yourself in communication with other human beings. It is the quality of that communication that determines the kind of person you become.

One unfortunate result of premature sex experience is that as soon as sex enters the relationship, other person-to-person communication diminishes. One couple found that they both so anticipated their intimate moments alone together at the end of the evening that they could not really enjoy a party, or other couples, or even one another. Their relationship had moved too fast to levels of intimacy that neither of them were truly ready for. It was not surprising to find them breaking off—as so often happens when sex relationships are not based upon mutual knowledge, respect, and devotion.

In marriage husband and wife become a new unity in which all they have been before is fused. Into their sex union flows all their common life together—their social, and emotional, and financial, and spiritual, and family interests and concerns. They come together feeling deeply that they belong to each other, as indeed they do. Their sexual communion is approved by society and blessed by their church. It expresses their status as a married pair ready now to establish a family into which children will come—as the end result of their creative partnership.

Personal Responsibility

One couple approaching marriage had this to say about why they had not had sexual relationships:

It is something we haven't really earned yet. We have no right to live together as man and wife until we are married. Until we marry we have no real responsibility for each other, in the eyes of the law and of our Lord. To us this is important enough to wait for, serious enough to postpone sex relations until we are truly one.

Others may not see the issue so clearly, nor feel so sure about what is wrong and what is right. Few can define exactly what other people ought to do in all circumstances. But there is one thing about sexual behavior upon which most reasonable men and women agree. There has to be a moral standard of some sort to regulate sexual relationships. An experience so profound in its effect upon both individuals and society as a whole cannot be left entirely to individual judgment.

It is irresponsible for two people to tell each other, "We can do what we please, and what happens is nobody's business." Such a stance takes no responsibility for their relationship, or for each other. It assumes no responsibility for their friends or families or for the child that may be conceived. Sexual union is personal and private, but it is also a relationship that has wide and deep social responsibilities.

Rabbi Joshua Loth Liebman, author of *Peace of Mind,* wrote:

> Can unchastity and incontinence be accepted as part of natural life? The answer must be that creative renunciation of evil is part of any decent life. The only mature form of human relationship between man and woman is monogamy. The adulterer, more than we suspect, is a tragic figure running from romance to romance, always lonely, frustrated and unhappy. Our age with all its so-called sophistication about sex and marriage is actually very shallow because it has not learned the lesson of saying no to certain impulses. As a rabbi, I believe that young people as well as adults must be summoned by religion to discriminate between the decent and the indecent, to achieve the mastery of self which comes when we realize that moral growth alone can give us inner serenity. Renunciation of immoral acts hurting both ourselves and other human beings in the circle of our influence is the true mark of maturity and nobility.

You cannot repeal the moral law. Chastity, morality, fidelity are virtues that have proven themselves through thousands of years of mankind's struggle. The wisdom of the ages is borne out in the lives of great men and women, living and dead. Growth of the human spirit is a product of self-mastery and personal responsibility.

You see irresponsible persons all around you. Their behavior reflects their values and their stage of development as yours does for you. As you cherish honesty, freedom, integrity, loyalty, and personal responsibility, these are the choices that control your sexual behavior. These will be the things you live by. The more nearly your standards parallel the laws of life, the better your life —and those influenced by you—will be.

The religious standard that puts sex within the fidelity and security of marriage is the most responsible code that has been developed. You need not expect it to be followed faithfully by everyone—no code ever is. You are justified in following it without apology today, as the best standard for protecting human, moral, and religious values that has yet been devised.

You are coming into maturity at the beginning of a new age. The moral revolution taking place all around you is a sign of the breaking up of old ground. Outside the city a farmer is plowing under last year's stubble in readiness for sowing this year's crops. As the soil breaks away from the plow, it crumbles on either side. The ground has to be loosened for the seeds of the new crop to take hold and grow. So it is with you and your life and your time in history. If you sow seeds of courage and of character in the moral soil of your times, you plant moral integrity in your future as a people.

You are a creature with a soul, as the human spirit you were designed to be. Man has always sought a purpose in his life beyond the here and now. He has not always reached this dream of being something more than flesh and blood, urge and impulse. It has not ever been an easy quest. Mankind has a history of groping for guidance in every age.

The hope ahead for you and yours lies in yourselves. Moral regeneration begins not in the pulpits but in the pews, not with the masses but within little groups of like-minded individuals. It starts in discussion of ethical values and meanings by people who care what happens. It gains momentum as your decisions make you stand tall and gain stature as persons. Its fruits are the personal and national character that result from disciplined commitment to the best that is known.

10
How Does It Affect Your

You dream of marriage as few others ever have. Studies show that American young people put being married and having a family first in their plans for the future. Not only girls, but fellows as well, look forward to being married, long before they are out of school. The chances are you have a pretty clear picture in your mind of the kind of life partner you will have and the type of home you will build. You probably see your children and how you will bring them up in your mind's eye right now. No question about it, you are marriage-minded.

You believe that marriage is worth waiting for. Boys and girls in schools enrolling married students are found to be more conservative about necking on their dates than are students in schools that prohibit married students. Most of you have some contact with married teen-agers, and so you, too, have undoubtedly been impressed with the serious outcome of intimate dating behavior.

You think that marriage should last for a lifetime. When your author asked some 3,500 high-school students across the country the question, "Do you think that marriage should last for a lifetime?" the overwhelming majority said "Yes." More than 90 per cent of the girls saw marriage as a permanent relationship. Although the boys were somewhat more skeptical, at least eight out of every ten in every school were convinced that marriage should last through life. The evidence is that American young people believe in marriage and take it seriously indeed.

You probably agree with Dr. Mary Steichen Calderone that there *is* a natural drive toward permanence that leads to marriage. You, too, sense that underlying your wish to please or to be popular or to have fun now is a deep yearning for a permanent relationship in marriage. This is so precious and so personal that you may not often put it into words. But articulated or not, this longing for a lasting companionship is fundamental and real. As Professor William E. Hulme puts it:

> Marriage is a companionship; not just an ordinary companionship, but the most intimate companionship of all. Marriage is a partnership; not just an ordinary partnership, but the most

Marriage, Your Family?

complete partnership of all. The helper fit for man is not simply a helper in this or that venture, but a helper in living. The mates share life together. It is the most creative togetherness in the world. Husband and wife in their union together bring forth new life. By becoming partners with each other they become partners with the Creator. The mates are honored with parenthood. So you can look forward to marriage as the most wonderful of all human relationships—and the most challenging.

A Happy Marriage Is Worth Striving For

A happy marriage does not just happen. It is the result of the coming together of two persons who care enough about one another and their marriage to work for happiness. Years ago, Professor Terman found that there was a direct relationship between premarital conduct and marital happiness. More husbands and wives who have not had sex experience before marriage were happily married than were those who had gone all the way before they were married. Of those men and women who had had premarital sexual intercourse, the more promiscuous they had been premaritally, the less likely they were to be happy maritally. This does not say that those who go the limit before marriage wreck their chances for happiness in marriage. But the Terman and other studies do definitely indicate a relationship between responsible sex conduct and happiness in marriage.

There is a clear relationship between coming to marriage as a virgin and not being tempted into adultery. Of the husbands Professor Terman studied, less than 10 per cent who married without premarital sex experience often felt the desire for extramarital intercourse. This is less than half the percentage (21.7 per cent) found among husbands who had known other women sexually before they had married. Men and women who have been permissive sexually before marriage cannot be expected to change miraculously when they marry. With few exceptions, they continue to manage their sex impulses as they did before they married. If adultery would not be serious to you, then premarital chastity may not matter so much. But if fidelity in marriage is important to you, then recognize that it is tied in with fidelity before marriage.

The remarkable thing in American marriage today is not that some break their marriage vows, but rather that so many remain faithful to their marriage partners. Now, when men and women move about so freely, with so many opportunities for playing around, fidelity in marriage might be expected to be rare indeed. But this is not the case. Studies agree that in America today approximately one-half of all husbands are faithful to their wives from their wedding day until they die. The vast majority of those who do make love to other women appear to do so in rather meaningless episodes rather than in ongoing relatively permanent attachments. Many men apparently prefer to love one woman exclusively rather than to seek variety in their sex partners.

Modern wives have much more freedom to do as they please than did their grandmothers. They obviously do not wish to get involved with other men to any alarming extent. Studies to date indicate that less than one in four American wives are ever unfaithful. Something there must be that keeps wives and husbands true to one another through the years. That something may be loyalty. It may be the sacred wedding pledge to cleave only to one another as long as they both shall live. It may be the personal commitment that marriage means to both men and women. It may be their mutual need for one another, and for the permanence their marriage means to them both.

The miracle of fidelity in marriage is the uniquely private climate in which married people can develop. It is the warmth that protects modern men and women from the chill of loneliness. It is the need for nearness, for closeness, and for companionship. It is the continuing dialogue of two who know each other's past and present and want to share their future. It is a healthy, happy way to live.

The head of a New York agency that books high-fashion models told one of her girls who was deep in some love tangle:

> Nothing will break down a woman's beauty faster than a love affair outside her marriage, whether it is because she's afraid of losing her husband or because she herself is leading a guilty life. The cosmetics inventor who discovers how to recapture the serenity of the happily married woman will become a millionaire overnight. There is no cream or powder in the world that can duplicate the kind of contented color and light that shines in a woman who knows she belongs to one man and that that man belongs to her.

Sex Belongs in Marriage

Two people of opposite sexes can create more enduring happiness in a permanent relationship than in any temporary affair. Their mutual pleasure in each other is more than instinct in action. Their satisfaction comes from learning to respond fully and completely to one another. Their response depends upon adjusting to each other mentally and emotionally as well as physically. Their full enjoyment as a couple therefore normally grows as they grow, and develops as they develop more and more experiences and interests in common.

Sexual intercourse reserved for marriage enjoys a maximum of security and privacy. The married couple are expected to live together as husband and wife. They enjoy their intimate moments with one another with a feeling that what they are doing is right, has the blessing of their family and friends, and the approval of society. They come together secure in each other and in their relationship. As a married couple they have privacy and permanence— two precious factors usually lacking in love affairs not blessed by marriage.

Married lovers come together free of guilt and shame. They have fewer qualms of conscience than do those who are haunted by the ghostly reminders of previous affairs. Jealousies born of comparisons with former partners are avoided by husband and wife who wait for marriage before being active sexually. It is a rare husband who is completely happy in the knowledge that his wife has slept with some other man before she married him. Even the most sophisticated lover is proud to marry a virgin whom he alone possesses. The predominant reaction of wives discovering their husbands' premarital experience with previous girl friends is unfavorable, according to Professors Burgess and Wallin. Sex reserved for marriage starts out with a clean slate upon which the married partners write their own love story in their own way from the beginning.

When sexual gratification is available only in marriage, it becomes unique. This special quality of the husband-wife relationship strengthens their union and stabilizes their marriage. Emotionally the two associate their sex life with marriage, and so are continually rewarded as they build their home together. Their thoughts are of each other as they develop a common past, and as they plan for a mutual future as wedded lovers. Such sex partners become partners in parenthood secure upon the strong foundation of marriage and family life.

Now when boys and girls and men and women share so much of each other's world in school and at work and in community activities, it makes sense to save sexual relations exclusively for marriage. Professor Kirkpatrick reports that couples who have engaged in premarital sexual relationships, not infrequently terminate their sexual intimacies before they marry so that they may enjoy a more dramatic transition from the single to the married state.

Numerous studies over the past thirty years find premarital chastity associated with both engagement success and marital adjustment. There are some with previous sex experience who make successful marriages. There is some evidence that physical sexual adjustment in marriage is somewhat related to sex experience. But there is more to a good marriage relationship than an immediately satisfactory sexual adjustment. In general, premarital chastity is a favorable beginning for a marriage, for one's own marriage adjustment, and for the happiness of one's marriage partner.

You want to be free to marry when *you* want to. You do not want to be trapped into anything as important as marriage is to you. You want the freedom to marry when you wish and whom you choose. No one really likes to have to do it. Your freedom of choice is directly related to your sexual responsibility. Fidelity to the marriage that will someday be yours, and to your future marriage partner, is the most reliable way of keeping free to choose.

When you marry, you want to be glad of it. You want to be pleased with each other. You want to be really happy about your love for one another. You want to be proud parents of your first baby. You sense even now that it is the feelings of love and mutual trust that open the floodgates of response between marriage partners.

"The happily married man regardless of age will find infinitely more satisfaction in a single sex act with his beloved than a boy of 18 can find in a dozen adventures with as many girls," says the psychiatrist Dr. Louis P. Saxe. For the woman, permanence and security are even more important for sexual satisfaction.

The simple conclusion is that intercourse is most meaningful when you are living together as husband and wife. Sex in marriage celebrates the simplest joy and symbolizes the most profound faith two people can know. As a unique thread through marriage, sex weaves significance into the warp and woof of everyday living in a way that is impossible otherwise. Sex belongs in marriage for the sake of continuing, complete fulfillment of man and wife, and for the sake of the marriage and family that it secures.

Secure Family Life

A healthy, secure family life is a life-and-death matter, says Dr. Gibson Winter. He goes on to point out that a society depends upon stable people to survive politically, economically, spiritually. Human beings become stable as they grow up in an atmosphere of love and order. Children of all ages need to know what to expect, even as you and I do. Men and women need concerned response from others in order to grow to their full stature as human beings.

Secure families provide the intimate relationships in which persons get to know one another. In a secure family the members support each other, identify their interests with one another, and grow in a climate of continuing love and affection. No other modern association offers so much to so many for so long a time.

It is families that produce children, care for them through infancy, train them for life, and protect them until they are ready to leave for homes of their own. Such a task should have top priority—that of literally making the men and women of tomorrow. Anything that strengthens families should therefore be encouraged. Anything that might endanger family life should be challenged.

Experienced homemakers have no question about the supreme importance of what they are doing. The University of Chicago has been studying what happens through the first twenty years of marriage. One finding is that there are significant shifts through the years toward more positive and favorable attitudes toward marriage, church, and child-rearing on the part of both men and women. Both husbands and wives agree that it is *not* a good idea to have sexual intercourse before marriage—an attitude that the researchers find constant through all twenty years from engagement through marriage.

Children have a right to be born into families that want them and are ready to love and care for them. Jerry found this out personally. He discovered just before his sixteenth birthday that he was born seven months after his parents had married. Not only that, but his coming panicked his father, who took off and left his young wife to fend for herself those first difficult months. In time the family was reunited, but the scars of those early days still sting. Jerry now has a serious attitude toward love and sex and marriage. He says with a determined voice:

> Believe me, when I get married, it will be when I am really ready to take care of a family. None of this chasing around for me. It is no way to bring a baby into the world. My son is

going to be proud of me because I am determined to be a good husband and father. This is important to me. Too important to throw away in some wild escapade or trivial love affair.

Sex Standards of the Family-minded

You find all kinds of sex standards around you today. There are the sexually irresponsible persons, who lack roots in intimate relationships or interest in permanent ties. There are those who emphasize "living it up" and "having fun"; they go all out for pleasure at any cost. There are some who insist that "all is fair in love and war"; these are frankly exploitative, even ruthless as lovers. There are those who honestly believe that love and sex are permissible so long as the two persons have a good relationship as a couple. Then there are the boys and girls and men and women who plan to keep their sexual activities exclusively within their marriage and family life.

Family-minded persons see sex as an essential and positive force in marriage. They care about families as necessary for personal and social well-being. They usually have deep roots and ongoing loyalties that make it possible for them to maintain fairly strict codes of behavior. They find security not only in each other but in striving toward their dream of an orderly, secure world built solid by stable families. Standards that limit sexual relationships to marriage are clear-cut and workable for them. When sex is restricted to marriage, everyone knows what to expect of himself and others. Being married is a clear distinction about which there is no question. It combines permanence and security, love and sex in a generating relationship that establishes and safeguards a family through the years.

Dr. David Mace puts the case for such a sex standard when he raises the question in a magazine article, "Is Chastity Outmoded?" to which he replies:

> There is not the slightest doubt in my mind as to the answer. Sex must be the servant of love, of parenthood, of home life. A sound code of sexual behavior, therefore, is one which leads to a state of society in which marriage and family living are happy and wholesome, stable and secure. The standards of sexual behavior in any community are to be measured by the quality of its home life. . . .
>
> What we need is a new idea of chastity, as a discipline gladly accepted so that human love can be kept warm and tender and unsullied. This idea of chastity means refusing to use

sex at subhuman levels and for selfish and antisocial ends. It is not the renunciation of sexual love as something evil. Rather it is the recognition that sexual love is something too good to be spoiled by misuse.

Your Parents and Your Sex Life

You have a two-way look at family life. You look forward to the family you someday will build when you get married. You review the family relationships you have known in the family you have grown up in through the years. You may find yourself saying at least to yourself at times, that when you grow up and have children, you will rear them differently than your parents have reared you. Just as surely, there are other aspects of your past family life that you want to continue in the home of your own. So, in a very real way the family you are now emerging from influences the family you will found as a husband or a wife, a father or a mother.

Your relationship with your parents is a powerful factor in the kind of sex standards you maintain. If you have had a warm, close relationship with your father and mother through the years, you tend to look for warmth and understanding in your friends, and certainly in your life partner. If you have felt loved and appreciated, you very likely have confidence in yourself now, and therefore you don't have to rush off into impetuous affairs just to get a little loving in your life. If you are able to talk things over at home, you find that problems do not loom so large nor get so tangled as when you just cannot get through to your parents with understanding.

If you find that you cannot seem to communicate with your parents as you once did, it is not a sign that anything is necessarily wrong with them, or with you. It may be simply that this is one way in which you are trying to emancipate yourself from your childish dependence upon your family.

A good many teen-agers are unable to get through to their parents with a sense of mutual understanding. Some feel so rejected, or neglected, or abused that they look for attention outside their homes. Others with a basic sense of trust and love for their parents at times feel enough annoyance and resentment to be in danger of hasty, defiant behavior.

H. H. Guest, Supervisor of Guidance for the Winnipeg Schools in Manitoba, outlines three suggestions for those times of angry rebellion:

1) Write out your feelings about your parents (on asbestos if

necessary) to reread a week or a month later, in order to see if these feelings are persistent or transient

2) Recognize how strong feelings push people into unreasonable acts; so don't *act* when you're stirred up

3) When you feel full of resentment and empty of acceptance at home, talk with an adult whose judgment and confidentiality you trust, who will listen, and who believes in you.

One of the hazards to avoid in growing up is going to extremes in declaring your independence. Emmy Lou felt so tied down by her father's heavy-handed bossiness that she got involved with a boy of whom she knew her family would disapprove, just to show that she could. This is not uncommon. Studies of girls who are in trouble indicate that sometimes an unmarried girl has a baby, not because she really loves the boy, but because she wants to get back at one or both her parents, who she feels are too strict, or too neglectful. The unfortunate thing is that it is not only the parents who are hurt by youthful indiscretions. It is the girl and the boy who bear the biggest burden when they get into trouble.

During your teens you become critical of your parents—more critical than you have been before or will be again. Other kids criticize their parents so much that it seems to be the thing to do. It gives you a feeling of being somebody in your own right, too, when you say something negative about the family that brought you up. At times your own behavior toward your parents may bewilder and bother you. Sally asks with tears brimming, "Why am I so mean to my own mother, who is the best friend a girl ever had?" At times you, too, may feel as Sally did and wonder why you act the way you do at home.

It may help to know that even while you are rebelling most decidedly against your parents, you appreciate them and respect them and love them too. In one study, three thousand Minnesota teenagers completed such sentences as, "My father is . . ." Both boys and girls expressed overwhelmingly favorable attitudes toward their parents. Another research study at the University of Chicago found that young people ascribe more favorable traits to their parents than to themselves, or even than their parents do to themselves.

You may rail against the controls that your parents set for you, but deep down inside you probably appreciate them. Studies of high-school students in Pennsylvania were made on how teen-agers and their parents feel about such conduct as drinking, smoking, failing in school, divorce, dancing, dating, and so forth. More of these young people evaluated their parents' points of view as "sensible" than either "too critical" or "not critical enough."

In Coleman's study, students in ten midwestern high schools were asked which would be hardest to take, as the result of joining a school club—the disapproval of one's parents or breaking with one's closest friend. Here again, it was the parents who received the majority vote. Some 53 per cent of the high-school students felt their parents' disapproval would be hardest to take, while 43 per cent said that breaking a friendship would matter most. This was a tough spot to put a teen-ager in, but it mirrors many a life situation. There are times when you, too, have to choose between going along with the crowd, or standing firm for what your parents have taught you to be right. If you are growing up well, you will conform to your friends' expectations in things that do not matter a great deal—in clothes and music and so forth, but in the things that really matter most, you will tend to follow your family's standards most of the time.

Nothing quite as sensitively gauges your family relationships as do your sex conduct and attitudes. When you are getting along pretty well with your parents, you go along comfortably with their dreams and ideals for you. When you break with them over some issue, you may be tempted to take out your hurt and your loneliness in something that they consider wrong. It is what you reproduce and what you repudiate in your family that best measures your maturity and stature as a person.

Your life is all of a piece. What you have been until now you cannot slough off as unimportant. You cannot cut off your roots any more than a rosebush can, and still flourish. Somehow, some way, you have to come to terms with your family and yourself as a member of that family in order to move freely and comfortably into the family of your future. You are fortunate if you have grown up in a fine, happy family, for that is the sort of family you will tend to establish yourself. You are not doomed if in some ways your family falls short of what you want for yourself. You can recognize the limitations of your past and start building strongly for the future. It will not help to blame your love and sex problems on your parents. It is your life, and you are responsible. Your parents did what they could for you. Now it is your turn to do what you can for yourself, and the marriage and the family and the children that someday will be yours.

11 What Happens To

A good reputation is a priceless asset. It opens doors to the future for you. Through a good reputation you may enter homes, have access to others, and be accepted among persons of all ages. A reputation for being trustworthy eases the way to scholarships and into many a special privilege. A reputation for being responsible leads to responsible positions in high places. A reputation for being respectable opens the way to courtship and marriage with a highly thought-of individual. A good reputation cannot be bought, but it is one of the most valuable things you can acquire.

A good reputation is easily lost. Of all the things there are to cloud over the brightness of a shining reputation, none is so simple as sex. Sexual vitality is a powerful force to cope with as you mature. Right now you are long on vigor and short on experience—a vulnerable combination. Like other impulses, your sexual energy demands expression. But more than other drives, it meets up with taboos and codes and confusions that tend to restrict it. You can lose your temper and have your tantrum excused as youthful immaturity. But a reputation for sexual indiscretion reverberates down the years—as many a politician has discovered. Give in to your impulses and you risk both your present and your future. The main problem is in managing your sex conduct in ways that protect your reputation and preserve your self-respect.

The Functions of Gossip

"If only boys could be trusted not to tell, a girl would feel protected." "If only people wouldn't gossip, a person's reputation would be safe." True, but the fact is that boys do kiss and tell, and people do talk—here as in every human circle.

Gossip has many functions. It is an effective way of gathering and distributing news. It serves to communicate information. It is a means of passing time and of cementing relationships. In its simplest form gossip is a type of recreation. Hostile gossip directed against the offender gives a group a common target for its aggressions. Gossip serves to uphold traditional standards as the nonconformist is brought into line. Gossip reflecting public opinion becomes a powerful social force. Then, there are personal motivations like the following.

Mrs. Grundy may express her moral indignation about so-and-

Your Reputation?

so's affair because she has always wanted to do the same thing but
never quite dared. Or the gossiper may be punishing himself for
doing the things that he most condemns in someone else. Sometimes the gossip is trying desperately to maintain his or her own
moral position. Gossip is one method an insecure person uses to
get attention. It is often used to bolster up an individual's uneasi-
ness about his own behavior—past, present, or contemplated. There
are many reasons why gossip is widespread. It is a fact of social
life, and often a painful personal problem.

Rebecca Birch Stirling concludes a study of gossip by saying
that reputations and lives have often been ruined by gossip. The
road of the sexual nonconformist is rarely a smooth one.

Exploitative Pressures and Persuasion

Much of the talk about sex conduct that you hear from other
young people is exploitative. A boy brags about what he got away
with on a date. A girl enjoys regaling her friends with how crazy
her boy friend is about her. Each sex exploits the other often in
mutually harmful ways.

The fellow who is trying to get a girl to go further in love-making
than she wants to uses many an argument that is not original with
him. Indeed, the line of persuasion is so stereotyped that a girl
can learn to recognize it and cope with it responsibly. A boy can
learn to spot the girl who is seductive. When his standards do not
include getting involved in such an intimacy, he can protect himself from the temptress.

The person who is kicking over the traces tends to be insistent
in pressuring others to join him. This is true in most walks of life
and at all ages. Remember how when you were young, the kids
who dared you to do something dangerous usually talked long
and loud about how brave they were? Recall how they taunted you
by yelling about what a sissy you would be if you did not enter
into the proposed adventure? So too, it is the teen-ager who flouts
traditional standards that pushes hardest for the support of others.
His or her need may be so great that the pressures upon others to
join him become insistent and demanding. He is the one most
likely to yell "Square" or "Chicken" at those who prefer not to
go along with his proposals.

Young people who live within accepted codes of conduct do not have to push others into their standards. Because they feel sure enough of themselves, they do not have to hold forth about how right they are. They may not even publicly acknowledge their convictions or confess their virginity. They remain silent while those who are breaking away from traditional standards sound off in dormitory and locker room with their dates and buddies.

The individual who is responsibly doing what makes sense to him does not have to prove himself all the time. His ego does not need propping up so much that he has to have others' constant support. He, or she, has a quiet confidence and does not have to push others around. The biggest argument comes from those who challenge conventional codes.

You do not have to go along with such pressures. You can understand the problem and the person without being thrown into behavior that is not for you. You can accept the individual who tries to persuade you to do something you do not want to do, without going along with the actual behavior. As you mature, you learn to recognize the pressures that are not in line with your values and goals. As you gain experience, you learn how to respond to the persuasive arguments that you cannot "buy." As a businessman has to turn down offers that do not appeal to him, or a housewife has to turn away salesmen whose goods are not for her, so you, too, must develp the skill to protect yourself from others' unacceptable proposals.

Arguments, Rationalizations, and Reasons

You will not be dating long before you run into an assortment of "reasons" why you should go all the way before marriage. Most of these are arguments designed to be tempting. Many are rationalizations that sound like bona fide reasons but are not. Some are reasonable reasons that have to be weighed carefully by couples who care deeply for each other and for their common future.

Arguments are slanted differently for boys and for girls. Studies show that some boys put pressure on other fellows "to go pick up some girls" with such arguments as "What's the harm, it's just for kicks," "You aren't a man until you prove that you can function like one," and, "It's just good healthy animal behavior that every fellow is entitled to." Usually the implication is that the fellow who does not go along is somehow "chicken." The boy who feels sure of his own standards meets such taunts with confidence, and simply says, "Sorry, fellows, I have to work tonight," or something equally firm and final.

Exploitative arguments that girls hear are of a subtler sort. The male (boy or man) on the make whispers of what a cute little dish she is, and how utterly irresistible he finds her. He may tell her how much he needs her love in his lonely, misunderstood life. He assures her that she "sends" him, in ways that are completely uncontrollable. If he is an experienced wolf, he extols her virtues and details her charms. He suggests that she "prove" that she loves him as much as he does her. Meanwhile his hands fondle more and more intimately in ways designed to relax her into readiness. When the girl pulls away and indicates her unwillingness to proceed, the exploitative fellow plays his ace and threatens her with the label "frigid." Since few girls want the reputation for being an "ice cube," this is a particularly difficult dilemma. She has a right to consider herself a real woman without having to be trapped into "proving it." Her only recourse is firmly to decline to be further involved, without making more of a scene than he has already precipitated.

Neither boys nor girls need feel compelled to go along with such unsavory arguments. They can be recognized for what they are—exploitative and potentially dangerous. The individual who accedes to such pressures endangers not only the present but also the future. The girl who gets the reputation for being "an easy make" finds the struggle more frequent and with more partners in time. The boy known as "a good-time Joe" soon finds himself confined to those who share his name and game.

Teen-agers are particularly vulnerable to the rationalizations that make sex experience seem all right. Through the years when boys and girls are emancipating themselves from their families, they are often in rebellion against parental authority. Then somehow it is easy to convince oneself that premarital sex experience will "show them" how adult one is. A sex affair seems like the one sure way of proving to one's parents that they cannot run one's life. In anger and in rebellion a teen-ager may do things designed to hurt his parents, only to find that it all too often boomerangs and hits him as well.

You are in a risky position whenever you lunge into questionable behavior to "show" someone anything. When you dash into a new romance to show your former sweetheart how little you care, you are doing just the opposite, and endangering yourself at the same time. Persuading yourself that what you now feel is the "real thing" is a transparent piece of rationalization. It is an all too common way individuals try to convince themselves that they have a right to do what is wrong.

Reasonable reasons are the most difficult to appraise, because they sound so plausible. A psychiatrist for unwed mothers says that one of the reasons girls give for getting pregnant is, "I was in love and hoped he would marry me." At times this reason comes from the boy, who pleads, "You love me, don't you? Then why not prove it?" The fallacy, of course, is that love is not tested or proved by sex experience. Love develops and is assured throughout a loving relationship of two persons who learn to care for one another in many ways.

Dr. Lester Kirkendall emphasizes the quality of a relationship as one basis for moral decisions:

> Whenever a decision or a choice is to be made concerning behavior, the moral decision will be the one which works toward the creation of trust, confidence and integrity in relationships. It should increase the capacity of individuals to cooperate, and enhance the sense of self-respect . . .

Unfortunately, as far as premarital intercourse is concerned, few persons or couples *know* for sure how they are going to feel after they have initiated sexual relationships before marriage. Their intimacy may or may not create trust and mutual confidence; it may result in distrust and decreased confidence. You have no way of knowing whether your own sense of self-respect will be enhanced or undermined by going all the way before marriage. There are some couples who feel that their relationship was strengthened by their premarital sex experience. There are others who just as honestly wish they had not consummated their union before they married. You have no way of knowing how you and your partner will react until it is too late to back up. There is a first time only once.

Many a girl needs the sense of permanence and security that only marriage can give before she can respond to her mate. For both members of the pair the expression of love in sex is a learned skill. It takes tenderness and patience and mutual devotion to make sex come alive. Like a language, fluency in sex expression improves with time. The married couple develop their own idioms and short cuts to getting through to each other that the unmarried couple can but rarely attain. A good sexual adjustment reflects a good relationship; it rarely precedes it.

"We *feel* married, so why not act as though we were?" is a

reason for premarital sexual relations that many a much-in-love couple has faced. They may have seen each other through a number of crises and become more devoted than ever. They may have been engaged for a long time. They may share so much of one another that they are a unit, a pair, inseparable. When that time comes, such a couple might well ask themselves, "If we feel that we truly belong to each other, why don't we get married and make it official?" The danger of acting as though they are married when in fact they are not is that they risk losing what they already have. Their relationship shifts into a new gear once sex intercourse is a part of their mutual experience. They may be able to weather the new emotional and social demands that their intimacy involves; they may not. Why take the chance?

Dangers of Delusion

The biggest danger of deluding yourself is that you begin to believe your own excuses. This happens in any scandal. A few years ago when the television quiz-show scandal broke, one of the officials insisted that no harm had been done, because everyone was happy.

The sponsor and his agency were very happy because they sold a great quantity of their product. The network was very happy because it had a top-rated show. Many of the contestants made more money than they ever expected. The unsuccessful contestants were happy to get on a national television program. And the television quiz audience was apparently happy because the shows were exciting.

Charles Van Doren, who enjoyed brief success as the key figure in this nationwide reputation-breaker, wrote his sentiments of the tragedy this way:

We tend to forget that we are moral agents, uniquely and individually responsible for what we do. To say, for example, to one who has erred, that most people would also have erred in the circumstances is no real consolation . . . *He is not all those other people; he is himself.*

This refusal to indulge in excuses and to attempt to justify his behavior was a measure of the stature of the man. But more, it protected Charles Van Doren from catching himself in the trap of his own setting. All too often when an individual has made a mistake, he is inclined to justify his behavior as "natural." He thereby places himself in with "those who do" as opposed to "those who don't." In premarital sex experience, this is a frequent occurrence.

It was Dr. Kinsey and his staff who made popular the categories of persons by their sex histories. In his classifications, anyone who had *ever* had sexual intercourse before marriage was classified among the premaritally sexually experienced. Into this category went not only the habitually promiscuous, but the devotedly monogamous, not only the individual with years of sex experience, but the one with a single episode to report. This mirrors the general definitions within our culture. The virgin is the individual who is yet to have complete sexual intercourse; all others are non-virgins. The harm in such labeling is that the person who once oversteps the bounds begins to see himself or herself as "sexually experienced." No longer seeing himself or herself as a virtuous person, the individual having gone the limit now identifies with the sexually sophisticated.

Classing oneself with those who have gone beyond bounds necessitates self-justifications. In order to live with this new image of oneself, the person rationalizes his conduct and excuses his behavior. Then it becomes increasingly difficult for the individual to see what he has done in perspective and to deal with his experience as a part of his total personality. He gives himself a reputation for sexual freedom that may or may not reflect his true nature. He judges himself guilty without benefit of judge or jury, in a land where every man is innocent until proven guilty. He develops negative feelings about himself and others, sometimes out of all proportion to what he or she has done.

Four Reputation-Conduct Equations

There are four possible combinations of reputation and conduct than can be put in predictable human terms: The first of these is:

(1) *Good reputation plus good conduct equals positive feelings about self and others.*

The individual who is well thought of by others, and who lives up to their faith in him, is not torn apart by inner conflict. He responds to others' favorable opinion of him with feelings of warmth and appreciation. He enjoys personal integrity and self-confidence. His feelings about himself and others are positive, and motivating. Not having to worry over how he appears to others, nor over his own anxieties about himself, he is free to love and to work and to play. This in essence is good mental hygiene.

You know many persons like this, effective, comfortable in their own skins, happy and content. As one student expresses it:

I have been choosing between courses of action since I was old enough to reason. My parents had confidence in me and my judgment from as early as I can remember. My friends and my church had the same high standards that my family held dear. There is no special virtue in my chastity. It is what I have chosen, as the way I want for my life. I believe in fidelity—to my parents' hopes for me, to my own sense of what is right, and to my future mate and marriage. What others call "fun" and "messing around" I would not find enjoyable. For I prefer keeping my life clean and open and above-board.

(2) *Good reputation plus poor conduct equals negative feelings about self.*

Let others down and you feel miserable. Take Marylou as an example. She grew up in a fine family, daughter of a prominent doctor. Her senior class in high school had listed her in their yearbook as "the girl most likely to go far." She was a good student, fairly attractive, active in church and school functions, one of those of whom everyone thought highly. Yet a few weeks before graduation the nurse found her trying to cut her wrists. Cornered, she admitted that she was pregnant, and that the man responsible was a married television repairman whom she scarcely knew. She felt so ashamed, death appeared to be the only way out. She sobbed that she had let everyone down—her parents, her classmates, her church, and her baby. Her humiliation was almost more than she could bear. She hated herself for what she had done and had already pronounced the death sentence upon herself for her crime. It took a long while for the psychologist to help her rebuild her faith in herself.

Not all cases of self-recrimination are so severe, but none are pleasant. There are few feelings more shattering than the sense of personal shabbiness in the face of others' confidence. There are reasons why an individual fails to live up to his or her reputation. As the person understands what made him behave as he did, the way back usually opens up with some hope for the future.

(3) *Poor reputation plus good conduct equals negative feelings about others.*

There are young people who struggle against almost impossible odds to gain a good reputation. Those who are condemned not by what they have done, but by how they appear to others easily fill with resentment at the unfairness of their lot. They feel hostile and hateful toward others whom they feel are not being fair. This sometimes is enough to make a delinquent out of a fellow.

Kids who grow up in poor neighborhoods are often made to feel unworthy. The son of an alcoholic father, the daughter of a mentally disturbed mother, children of a family that is suspect, are apt to live under a cloud not of their making. Such a youngster often reacts to being judged "bad" unfairly, by resenting and hating others. Until he can feel that there is a chance of being rescued from an unjustly poor reputation, his negative feelings are hazards to himself and others.

(4) *Poor reputation plus poor conduct equals negative feelings about self and others.*

Whatever one's background, a teen-ager may break the rules. The result is a bad reputation in the community and diminished self-respect. Here is the way one unhappy mixed-up teen-age girl expressed her predicament:

> People are plain rotten if you ask me. They can't wait for a chance to take out their meanness on a girl and that is what they are doing to me right now. They are making me feel like dirt. Just because I have more dates and boy friends than other girls, they hate my guts. I'm not pretty like other girls so I can't rely on my looks to get a date. I try to be more fun than other girls so the fellows will like my company. I can't let them think I'm poor funny-looking me from the wrong part of town. They wouldn't give me a second look unless I let them have what they want.
>
> Having so many fellows after me, I keep hoping that maybe one will want to be my steady and marry me as soon as I finish school. Only it never happens. I get so mad! They all seem to like making love to me, and then after once or twice that's the last I see of them. Then I go out with somebody else, and somebody else after that.
>
> I suppose word gets around. You know how sneaky boys can be. They probably whisper to each other how easy I am. So now folks have stopped talking to me. They turn the other way when they see me coming, and call me a tramp behind my back. The nice girls at school won't have anything to do with me. They all are just plain jealous, but they say I'm no good. . . .

The psychologist whose case this is told the girl to stop being sorry for herself, and to face up to the fact of her bad reputation without blaming others for what she had done to herself. Then she can take the next step toward finding herself as a person with a future. Like the young man in the movie who said he used to be "Nobody going nowhere," the person whose conduct and reputation need improvement has to find his way back to believing he is Somebody.

Finding Your Way Back

Everyone makes mistakes at times. Instead of wallowing in feelings of guilt, or pretending you enjoy being "bad," you can learn from your mistakes. You can learn to live with yourself and others. You can become more compassionate toward others' weaknesses once you have learned from experience that "to err is human."

The first step in finding your way back to self- and others' acceptance is to face up to the facts. Recognize that you have done wrong, that you have hurt your good name, that you have been a fool. It may not be easy to get over the hurdle you have made for yourself, but it can be done, and *you* have to do it.

This means that you cannot afford to make excuses for yourself. Blaming others for what you have done will not help. You must accept responsibility for your own behavior. When you do not like your conduct, you can determine not to repeat this kind of thing again. As Jesus told the woman taken in adultery, "Go, and sin no more."

Self-understanding rather than self-condemnation is the way to inner peace and self-respect. Remind yourself of your strong points —your mind, your body, your spirit, your determination to succeed. Face your weaknesses, but do not give in to them. Accept your own life—both your strengths and your limitations—as the foundation upon which you must build your future.

Explore what it was that made you do what you did just then. You may find, as others have, that difficulties in controlling the sex impulse arise when other aspects of life are out of kilter. As you get the rest of your life straightened out, your sex drive becomes more manageable. In the meantime, you are wise to get busy at the adjustments that are making life hard for you right now.

It probably will help you to talk out your problems. Confide in some worthy adult in whom you have confidence. Your minister, a trusted teacher, your school guidance worker may help you to the perspective you need. Most parents are more understanding than is generally recognized. Your own father and mother may be a real source of strength to you now. Finding a responsible individual to hear you out can give you a real boost out of your despair with yourself.

It may be that the partner of your guilt can be a confidant. One girl reported, "I was only tempted to go too far once. But we stopped in time, and then spent two hours talking it over. He wanted to be a doctor, and we both knew we just didn't want to spoil our futures. So we've been dating each other without trouble ever since." The beauty of this case is that both persons, and their relationship with one another, were strengthened as they faced their struggle together.

Somewhere along the way ahead you will find that you can forgive yourself. Without rationalizing your behavior, or excusing your conduct, you can trust yourself once more. This becomes possible as you realize that you try to measure up to your own and others' expectations as best you can. There are times when you do not quite meet your own or others' standards. Then you must develop your strengths in the areas where you fell short, so that the hazard that tripped you can be surmounted another time. If it was others' expectations that conflicted with your personal goals, your challenge is "to thine own self be true."

Finally, it is up to you to start afresh, on another track. Make a clean break with the conduct that got you into trouble. Align yourself with the causes and the groups than can help you rebuild your life along more positive lines. Become active in your church. Volunteer for some service project in your neighborhood. Associate quietly and humbly with good people and worthy activities. Make your life and your time count for something. The chairman of the Executive Committee of the Menninger Foundation puts the challenge this way:

> If each of us can be helped by science to live a hundred years, what will it profit us if our hates and fears, our loneliness and our remorse will not permit us to enjoy them? What use is an extra year or two to a man who "kills" what time he has?

Your character is the sum total of what you stand for. Your reputation reflects what you fall for. The two go together, mirroring your life as long as you live.

12 How Do You See Yourself?

What you do about your sex life depends upon how you see yourself. If you have developed a positive, forward-looking self-concept, you keep your conduct in line with your dreams. If you have become discouraged about yourself, you may feel, "What's the use?" and snatch what satisfactions you can find — sexually and otherwise.

You tend to do and to be what is expected of you, if you can. You try to measure up to those standards that your family and your friends set. You cannot do *everything* that others want you to do—ever. You do conform to those expectations that advance your own developing sense of yourself.

More than anything else, your sense of identity determines your goals and aspirations, dreams, and hopes. Therefore, the most important thing right now for you is developing positive feelings about your life and what you are going to do about you.

Who Do You Think You Are?

Who are you? You speak your name, but what does that mean to you? You are a member of your family, with all that means in identifying yourself. You belong to various friendship groups, clubs, and organizations, toward which you have varying degrees of loyalty. You are a student, whose achievements are graded and known. You have some skills and abilities, which help place you in your own estimation as well as others'. Certain people count upon you for responsibilities and services, of which you are proud, resentful, or indifferent. Your self is the person you see yourself to be, mirrored in the eyes of those who know you.

You build your sense of identity over the years. A good sense of your self is an achievement that fits your potentials and your life situation. As you see yourself clearly, you find answers to life's most perplexing questions: "Who am I? What kind of person am I really? Where am I going? What am I going to be?" This helps you find a place in the world of which you are a part. It gives you a basis for making decisions that otherwise would be difficult.

Young Red is a good illustration. He greatly admired his uncle, who was a prominent doctor. Red wanted to become a physician like him—a dream in which his uncle encouraged him. He studied and worked toward his goal of getting into medical school. One night, when some of his classmates drove by on their way "to pick up some girls and have fun across town," it was not hard for Red to bow out of their invitation to come along. He saw himself as the kind of person who did not "make out" with some girl from across the tracks. He recognized that his sexual conduct was a part of his life and not just an isolated episode. He therefore behaved as he believed a future doctor should.

Dr. Erik Erikson stresses how important it is for a young person to establish his own sense of identity before he or she becomes intimate with another. He sees your major problem as "identity crisis" now when you are faced with so many different models of what to become. Out of these confusions you must work through your own sense of self before you are ready to merge yourself with another human being in true intimacy. Until you know who you are, you cannot express yourself with confidence. Only as you emerge from your struggle to find yourself, can you attain mutuality of sexual fulfillment with a beloved partner of the other sex.

You do not discover who you are all at once. You gain your sense of identity a bit at a time through the years. Life is a series of recurring struggles in which you succeed or fail, each time with the possibility of seeing yourself more clearly than you had done before. Your sense of who you are does not suddenly appear out of the blue. It evolves out of your daily response to life. Now that you are more and more on your own, your big task is to manage yourself in terms of your emerging sense of who you are, what you want out of life, and how you feel about your relationships with others.

Once you know what you want to do about your sex standards, your next step is to learn how to put them into practice. You then face at least four questions: 1) How do you know when you are really in love? 2) How far should you go in expressing your feelings? 3) How do you stop without hurting yourself or your partner? 4) How do you build a person-to-person relationship that is deeply meaningful and lasting? These and other related questions are considered in *Love and the Facts of Life* (author and publisher the same as this book's).

As you find yourself, you realize that you cannot experience everything. You cannot attack others without punishment. You cannot express all your feelings and get along with other people—or with yourself. You learn to control your impulses of the moment for future fulfillment. You have faith that the best things in life are worth waiting for—and become more meaningful because of your restraint.

No One Is Perfect

You have made many mistakes. You have done things that you knew were wrong. The chances are some memories of your past behavior make you blush with shame. It is the way in which you face these parts of yourself that you are not proud of that make a difference in your future sense of yourself.

Dr. Poffenberger's study of 1,200 high-school students found both boys and girls at times did things that were counter to their moral principles. Like them, you some time may have been so rebellious that you went out and deliberately did something that you knew was wrong. Because you were bored and unhappy about yourself, you went along with some out-of-bounds escapade that really was not your idea of a good time at all. These things happen to a teen-ager from time to time.

Making a really bad mistake and doing something that offends your own sense of what is right is unfortunate. But even worse is convincing yourself that you are the kind of person who stands for that kind of thing. When you get into a sex jam, for instance, you can (1) convince yourself that because others are doing the same thing, you too have the same right; or (2) assume responsibility for your mistake and take steps to avoid that particular hazard another time.

Do something wrong and you feel sullied. Your shame and guilt make you uncomfortable. It is easy then to convince yourself that you meant to do what you did in the first place. You flaunt your behavior defiantly, as many others around you are doing. The louder you talk, the more convinced you become that what is wrong is right. In time you alienate yourself from the persons you really admire. Your new sense of who you are is bolstered up by the bragging support of your new friends. Your lot is cast among those who see themselves as you do. You condemn yourself to live cheaply because you do not know how to value your best self. Stephen Spender tells of how he drove himself into just such a corner:

> My revolt against the attitude of my family led me to rebel altogether against morality, work and discipline. Secretly I was

fascinated by the worthless outcasts, the depraved, the lazy, the lost, and wanted to give them the love which they were denied by respectable people. This reaction was doubtless due to the fact that I wanted to love what I judged to be the inadmissible worst qualities in myself . . . I had driven myself and had been driven into a kind of sexual slum.

Dr. Celia Deschin's work with teen-agers who had contracted venereal disease led her to see that promiscuity may be related to lack of goals and rootlessness. Young people with no vision of what they can become easily get discouraged and take the line of least resistance. A boy (or a girl) who has a dream of what lies ahead learns to pick himself up when has stumbled and get going again.

It takes personal courage to admit that you have been wrong. But this is the direction of growth and development. You realize how easy it is to do the things that are unworthy of you—especially in sexual conduct. But when you have done something that you are sorry about, you admit it with regret. You do what you can to make amends for your unfortunate behavior. You face the future stronger in this particular area because you have admitted your weakness.

Sally is admired by all who know her. Yet she once was terribly discouraged. She was the fourth illegitimate child in her family. Her mother had a series of lovers through the years one of whom had been her father—which one her mother was not sure. When she was barely twelve, an older man tried to take advantage of Sally, and she almost let him. Just in time she screamed for help and ran away—to a new life. Now she is being graduated from high school, a popular, attractive girl, whose future looks bright. In telling her counselor about the change in her life that came the moment she realized that she was about to repeat her mother's life pattern, she said, "I wanted something better than Mother ever had. I wanted to get out of all that, and make a good, clean life for myself."

Sally had more of a handicap to overcome than most of us have. Yet each of us bears the burden of our own and our family's weaknesses. We either succumb to them, or we rise above them. It all depends upon the ways in which we react to what happens, and what we really want to do about it. Surmounting guilt leads to fulfillment, and transcending shame leads to a sense of identity and freedom. As Dr. Helen Lynd puts it:

. . . the tragic limitations of man's fate remain. Any search for identity that ignores them is taking place in a meager or an unreal world. It is only with full awareness of these necessities that men can transform shame, affirm their pride, and continue their search for significance.

A Sense of Self You Can Live With

You have to live with yourself. Somehow or other you must become comfortable in your own skin. During your teen years you are finding out what it means to be a member of your own sex. Hopefully, you are learning to enjoy being a boy or a girl.

Dr. Martin Loeb finds that teen-agers who have learned to be comfortable in their appropriate sex roles are least likely to get involved in indiscriminate sexuality. Boys who enjoy being boys and look forward to becoming men trust themselves for what they are. Girls who like being feminine and anticipate becoming women, wives, and mothers can rely upon their own feelings. There is evidence that teen-agers who trust themselves are least likely to be involved in irresponsible sexual activity.

You develop a sense of self as you identify with a member of your own sex that you admire and want to be like. Usually this is a member of your family. But if you do not want to follow your parent's pattern, you look to some other worthy adult to model yourself after. Sally, in the case above, repudiated her mother's way of being a woman. She modeled herself, instead, after a favorite teacher who encouraged Sally to find herself.

Some of the qualities that you see in your family and in your closest friends, you like, and so you reproduce them as a part of yourself—almost without realizing it. Other things they do, you repudiate as you establish a sense of your own identity.

Your personal identification is always in relation to somebody and something. You find out who you are in relation to whom, and to what. One of our studies finds that teen-agers who do not want a marriage like their own parents' are more often in love with some special person than are those whose marriage dreams follow their parents' patterns. The indication is that to identify, you either feel at home in your parents' way of life, or you feel close to some personal friend with whom you can identify.

Dr. Jerome Himelhoch reminds us that the Kinsey studies found that boys usually learn the sex ways of their class of destination—not of their class of origin. Thus, once the boy identifies with a "group to which he only aspires and in which he does not have membership, he takes over its general mores, including those governing sexual behavior."

It is hard to refuse something that looks like fun and that others seem to enjoy. Yet it would be even harder to do something that is not appropriate to the self you see yourself becoming. Sometimes you are helped by talking over your confusions about sex with an adult in whom you have confidence. At times it helps to discuss your dilemmas about sex standards with friends of your own age. In the last analysis, you have to find out how you personally feel 'way down deep inside yourself.

The director of the Graduate Institute of Education at Washington University is quoted as saying:

> Only when a girl is forced onto herself, when she has to strike out on her own without the protection of group approval, only then do you get an expression of moral purpose or creativity. That's when she begins to discover who she really is.

You, too, may have already discovered that you cannot go along with the gang in all things indefinitely. You cannot blindly follow your family patterns in all ways for all time. There comes a time when you must pull away far enough from both your family and your friends to discover how you yourself really feel about the big issues of life. As you develop your own sex standards, an inner security safeguards you from outside pressures.

As Dr. Lester Kirkendall says in his article on "The Problems of Remaining a Virgin":

> I am convinced that any girl of reasonably firm character could preserve her virginity quite easily . . . she should feel that boys will respect and appreciate a girl who knows her own mind. Then, if she wishes to retain her virginity she should know why. She must be convinced that this is what she wants to do. And then she must make a plain, simple statement concerning her wishes at the appropriate time.

Those who have the most sexual difficulty are uncertain about their own standards. Fellows who advocate premarital sex experience for themselves hesitate to say they would give their own children a green light on the same behavior. When asked if he favored youthful sex experience, a university student replied, "For me or my kid sister?" Such a decision must come from a sure sense of who you are, and why.

Bases for Responsible Decisions

Now, when so many contradictory philosophies of life are being discussed, it is not easy to find your own best course. Since what you are becoming cannot be separated from the decisions you make about what you do and do not do, you need sound bases for these decisions.

One basis for decision-making is possible *outcome*. In your own experience, what happens as a result of premarital sexual relations? To your knowledge, what are the chances of something good coming out of such behavior? Something bad? How good? How bad? What reliable evidence is there that you can base your judgment on? Are you acquainted with the findings of valid research on this question? Have you talked over the problem with an informed responsible person who knows you and what you are deciding?

Your decision should be based upon possible outcome in terms of your own sense of what is appropriate. Since there are many life styles, and many kinds of persons, each must resolve the issue in terms of his or her own values and self concept.

One simple way of testing your own reaction is to envisage how you would feel if your conduct were reported in the newspapers. If you were a Jacqueline Kennedy, or an Elizabeth Taylor, or any of those whose every move is publicized, how would you feel about your own headlines? Would what you are contemplating doing make you pleased and proud? Or would you feel ashamed and guilty?

A second basis for moral decisions is that of *universality*. Ask yourself what would it be like if everyone did just what he or she felt like. If every boy took any girl who was available, what kind of world would it be? If couples engaged freely in premarital intercourse, what assurance would they have of fidelity after they married? If husbands and wives were not faithful to each other, what kind of family life would result? How could a man be sure his children were his? How could either of them feel permanently secure in their life together? Would women, would men, be better off or worse? Would marriages be happier or under more strain? How would children fare? What kind of culture would result? Does sexual restraint make a stronger or a weaker society?

Dr. J. D. Unwin, the British scholar, studied eighty civilizations ranging over the past four thousand years. He was impressed with the fact that a society chooses either sexual promiscuity and decay, or sexual discipline and creative development. He concludes, "Any human society is free to choose either to display great energy or to enjoy sexual freedom; the evidence is that it cannot do both for more than one generation."

The father of psychoanalysis came to the same conclusion. In his *New Introductory Lectures on Psychoanalysis,* Sigmund Freud wrote:

> We believe that civilization has been built up by sacrifices in gratification of the primitive impulses, and that it is to a great extent for ever being recreated as each individual repeats the sacrifice of his instinctual pleasures for the common good. The sexual are amongst the most important of the instinctual forces thus utilized: they are in this way sublimated, that is to say, their energy is turned aside from its sexual goal and diverted towards other ends, no longer sexual and socially more valuable.

A third basis for developing premarital sex standards is *cultural.* Dr. Leuba suggests that a culture in which premarital sexual intercourse would be desirable and satisfactory would have to meet the following conditions:

1. If guilt and shame were not associated with premarital sex expression in childhood-upbringing.

2. If there were no social disapproval either for the persons engaging in premarital sexual relations or for the institutions of which they were members.

3. If young people reaching puberty were well informed regarding the basic male and female sexual makeup and regarding socially acquired sexual attitudes.

4. If privacy were readily available; and sexual functioning were successfully restricted within satisfactory limits.

5. If universal and competent training in contraception were available.

6. If young people were brought up to take sex neither too seriously nor too lightly.

7. If social life were such that it would be easy for women as well as for men to become well acquainted with many members of the opposite sex, so that a woman, for instance, who had lost a partner would be able to find a new and equally satisfactory one without being left stranded or drifting into promiscuity.

8. If venereal diseases were rare or nonexistent.

9. If provisions were made for the care of offspring.

We would add to this listing three further conditions:

10. If religious teachings approved of premarital and extramarital sexual relationships.

11. If human-development findings indicated that adolescent sex

experience encourages the full development of the personality of both partners.

12. If premarital sexual conduct promoted the development of the family and the culture.

A reviewer would be optimistic indeed to convince himself that these conditions are being met in America today! Go down the listing yourself and see whether you can honestly appraise any of these twelve conditions necessary for premarital sexual intercourse as being met here and now.

Getting Involved—in What?

You are growing up at a time when you can get involved in almost anything—or nothing. From watching and reading about other people, you have become aware of all the many ways of living a life. Now you are at a time of your life when you are deciding in what you want to get involved, and to what you want to give yourself.

There are a good many young pairs who are getting involved with each other at early ages. At least for some boys and girls, dating begins even before they get into their teens. "Going steady" takes place at younger ages, and at earlier points in the relationships, than formerly. Very young daters often "go steady" for mutual support and security. They lean upon one another when they are not yet sure of themselves as persons. If you have felt rejected or neglected, you, too, may have gotten involved in a love affair before you were really ready for it.

"Making out" is not just a way of testing or expressing affection. It is often a game in which a person sees how far he can go with a sex partner he, or she, hardly knows. It is a risky way of showing how irresistible one is. It is a rather childish way of proving how grown up you are. It is frequently exploitative, and it not infrequently leads to trouble.

More marriages of teen-agers take place now than formerly. Studies show that early marriage is related to early dating, going steady, and "making out." When others are getting married while you are still in school, you may wonder if you should too. You may ask yourself what's wrong with getting married as soon as you can. Isn't that what most girls and fellows want? is the argument. Then why not? What's the harm?

The harm in early marriage is that you take on a difficult and important responsibility before you are really ready to settle down. You feel trapped when you marry too soon. Here are the ways four different fellows and girls put their early-marriage predicaments:

"What do I want with a baby? I haven't had any fun yet," says a seventeen-year-old wife and mother a few months following her "have-to" marriage. And a young husband says with regret:

It's almost too much to expect of a fellow to go to school, work, and try to be a husband and father too. I almost lost out in everything that mattered. I couldn't study and so nearly flunked out of school, and then my wife took the baby and went home to her mother. I just wish I hadn't gotten in so deep so soon.

An eighteen-year-old girl, in a premarital conference with her pastor, said, "I don't know what I am doing here. I want to travel. I want to go to college and make something of myself before I get married. But how do I keep from getting tied down now when I'm already so involved?"

"My girl is pregnant. Do I have to marry her?" is the poignant query youth leaders hear from many a lad. A responsible fellow feels like a cad even to consider walking out on a girl whose pregnancy he has caused. But when such a marriage cuts short his education, limits his vocational possibilities, and traps him before he has made a life for himself—what then?

The danger of getting involved sexually too soon is that you find yourself committed before you find yourself. This cuts short your further development as an individual, and it is not a good way to start your marriage. Marriage is not child's play. It is a real responsibility, calling for genuine maturity. This is one reason why teen-age marriages often fail—in divorce, separation, annulment, and in personal distress and disillusionment.

One reaction to early involvement is to avoid commitment at all costs. This is the "play it cool," "don't get tied down," "don't get caught," "don't get involved" advice you hear today. It is all part of the "don't sweat" syndrome that comes as a reaction to the dangers of too early involvement. It tends to be self-centered and exploitative as indicated in such typical admonitions as:

> "Keep 'em guessing."
> "Love 'em and leave 'em."
> "Look out for Number One."
> "Do as you please—just don't get caught."

Illustrative of this trend of avoiding involvement are recent news stories: the thirty-eight neighbors who saw a murder but did not call the police; the group who watched a girl being raped and beaten but did not try to help her; the adults who witnessed a five-year-old boy drowning in a pool, while even an experienced swimmer stood by and let it happen. When these people were asked why they did nothing to help right such wrongs, each said in essence, "I did not want to get involved."

Psychiatry and religion agree that your own well-being depends upon your involvement with others. You cannot live as though you were all there is. You have to belong to someone, to something, somehow, in order to survive as a person.

If you want neither to get prematurely involved sexually, nor to adopt the beatnik noninvolvement attitude, there is still another alternative. You can become committed to causes worth serving. The popularity of exchange students' programs and foreign-service projects such as the Peace Corps attests to youth's eagerness to serve. You find yourself, as you get involved in activities worth doing. You make something of yourself as you get training at the highest level of your competence. You do not have to throw your life away. You can find it in the life style that makes you feel significant.

Becoming committed means finding a social world in which you are at home. There are many social groupings in schools and colleges today. There is the sports crowd, who give themselves to "the game." There are the good-time Joes and Janes, who spend their time having fun. There are the hoods, the beatniks, malcontents, drop-outs—blindly rebelling against something, heading into they know not what. There are the students who have their eyes on academic excellence and scholastic achievement. There is the religious and service-oriented fellowship of church-related young people.

You need have no apology for being "one of the good kids." Chances are that if you are a good student, you will go further than some of the kids who are "goofing off." Studies show that religious teen-agers tend to grow up to become adult leaders. Getting involved in worth-while causes that are bigger than you are takes you out into the world of worthy people of all ages. Then your sex life becomes a meaningful part of your total fulfillment.

There always have been some boys and girls who went all the way before marriage. But there used to be little question about the virtue of chastity. Now an individual who prefers to wait until marriage before becoming sexually intimate faces pressures in the other direction.

If you choose to discipline your sex drive, you have plenty of company in the many persons of both sexes who also want to wait till marriage. You have the same kind of basis for your restraint that you accept when you enter the discipline of medicine or science or engineering or teaching. You play the game of life according to the generally accepted rules—as you do in athletics or business or highway-driving. In none of these can individuals do just as they please. In order to get where they want to go, people have to keep their behavior within bounds.

Morality is a set of rules that a society sets up to protect itself and its members. Your morals are the personal rules that you live by. They reflect who you think you are, and where you are trying to go. You might have more freedom without any restrictions. But traffic lights enable everyone to cross an intersection faster than they otherwise would. Waiting until marriage provides a smooth, safe road to the future.

Heather Banks, a teen-age girl, wrote in a recent issue of *The Atlantic Monthly:*

> Many of today's young people have high moral and ethical standards. Virtue has not gone out of style. My own experience shows that today's youths want chaste mates, spiritually as well as physically. I fail to see the distinction between a shotgun wedding and a hurry-up nuptial with a boy who farms out his fraternity pin so that he can "hop into bed". . .
>
> No wonder these girls cannot give their husbands everything. They have been doling out portions to Tom, Dick, and Harry. They have found no purpose in life, and so cannot plan to follow one. I wonder how they will feel when, at fifty, they turn back to reassess their youth.
>
> I am no prissy old maid. I am a sixteen-year-old girl who will enter college next Fall.

The American dream is a living, changing, growing thing that is no better and no worse than each of us who holds it in trust. Our nation is being continually re-created for better or for worse by people like you and me. There are some observers such as May Craig, celebrated correspondent in our nation's capital, who feel that we are in a desperate plight morally. She warns, "Unless there is a change, deep down, in the American people, a genuine crusade against self-indulgence, immorality public and private, then we are witnesses to the decline and fall of the American Republic." For some young people this is a burdensome challenge. For others it is a summons to greatness. Your life is built over the years by the answers you find to the kinds of questions considered here. The spirit of your world is created and re-created by people like you. Your personal decisions express your faith in yourself, and in your whole human encounter.

References

CHAPTER 1—What Are Your Sex Standards?

BLAINE, GRAHAM B., M.D. "Moral Questions Stir Campuses." *The New York Times,* January 16, 1964, pp. 73 and 85.

BROWER, CHARLES H. "The Return of the Square." An address before the Illinois State Chamber of Commerce, October, 1962.

CALDERONE, MARY STEICHEN, M.D. *Sexual Energy—Constructive or Destructive.* Paper given before the Academy of Psychosomatic Medicine, Tenth Annual Meeting, October 17, 1963, San Francisco, California.

DUVALL, EVELYN MILLIS. *Love and the Facts of Life.* New York: Association Press, 1963.

DUVALL, EVELYN M. and SYLVANUS M., eds. *Sex Ways—In Fact and Faith.* New York: Association Press, 1961.

EHRMANN, WINSTON W. *Premarital Dating Behavior.* New York: Henry Holt and Company, Inc., 1959.

GARDNER, JOHN W. "On Men and Moral Values." *Reader's Digest,* March, 1964, p. 168.

KIRKENDALL, LESTER A. *Premarital Intercourse and Interpersonal Relationships.* New York: The Julian Press, 1961.

"Morals on the Campus." *Calendar,* Columbia Broadcasting System network program, January 24, 1963.

MUELLER, KATE HEVNER, ed. "Student Sex Standards and Behavior: The Educator's Responsibility." *Journal of the National Association of Women Deans and Counselors,* XXVI, No. 2 (January, 1963).

"Open Letter to the Young Men and Women of Southampton's Debutante Party, An." *Chicago Maroon,* May 8, 1964, p. 12.

"Opportunity for Useful Community Role Cited as Teenage Need by Dr. Deschin." *Social Health News,* May, 1961, p. 2.

PEALE, NORMAN VINCENT. "What's Happening to Sex in America?" *Guideposts,* July, 1964, p. 5.

REISS, IRA L. *Premarital Sexual Standards in America.* Glencoe, Illinois: The Free Press, 1960.

SCHAUFFLER, GOODRICH C., M.D. "Today It Could Be *Your* Daughter." *Ladies' Home Journal,* January, 1958.

"Vassar Warns Girls, Behave or Withdraw." Associated Press release, Poughkeepsie, New York, May 8, 1962.

CHAPTER 2—Everyone Does It—or Do They?

BURGESS, ERNEST W., and WALLIN, PAUL. *Engagement and Marriage.* Philadelphia: J. B. Lippincott Co., 1953.

CHRISTENSEN, HAROLD T., and CARPENTER, GEORGE R. "Timing Patterns in the Development of Sexual Intimacy." *Marriage and Family Living,* XXIV, No. 1 (February, 1962), pp. 30–35.

———. "Value-Behavior Discrepancies Regarding Premarital Coitus in Three Western Cultures." *American Sociological Review,* XXVII, No. 1 (February, 1962), pp. 66–74.

DUVALL, EVELYN MILLIS. "Exploring Student Attitudes about Dating." *Journal of Home Economics,* LVI, No. 2 (February, 1964), pp. 86–88.

DUVALL, SYLVANUS M. "Facts and Fictions about Sex." *Look,* April 12, 1960.

———. "Sex Relations and the Family." *Religious Education,* LVIII, No. 2 (March-April, 1963), pp. 194–199.

EHRMANN, WINSTON W. "Influence of Comparative Social Class of Companion upon Premarital Heterosexual Behavior." *Marriage and Family Living,* XVII, No. 1 (February, 1955), pp. 48–53.

———. *Premarital Dating Behavior.* New York: Henry Holt and Company, Inc., 1959.

GERLING, AMY G. "Conflicts between Generations in Moral Norms." Presented at the 1961 Conference of the National Council on Family Relations.

KANIN, EUGENE J. "Male Sex Aggression in Dating-Courtship Relations." *The American Journal of Sociology.* LXIII, No. 2 (September, 1957), pp. 197–204.

KINSEY, ALFRED C., *et al. Sexual Behavior in the Human Female.* Philadelphia: W. B. Saunders Co., 1953.

———. *Sexual Behavior in the Human Male.* Philadelphia: W. B. Saunders Co., 1948.

REEVY, W. R. "Adolescent Sexuality." Albert Ellis and Albert Abarbanel, eds. *The Encyclopedia of Sexual Behavior.* New York: Hawthorn Books, Inc., 1960, pp. 52–68.

REISS, IRA L. *Premarital Sexual Standards in America.* Glencoe, Illinois: The Free Press, 1960.

"Sex Behavior Classified in Six Patterns." New York Times-Chicago Tribune Service. *Chicago Tribune,* November 14, 1963, page 8, Section 2A.

STEINER, GARY, and ARNOLD, GARY. *Feedback: Sex and Morals.* Chicago: WBBM TV, June 17, 1964.

"Strength in Numbers." *Time,* February 8, 1963, psychiatry section, p. 38.

CHAPTER 3—It's Natural

BARRON, JUDGE JENNIE LOITMAN. "Too Much Sex on Campus." *Ladies' Home Journal,* January–February, 1964, pp. 48 and 52. By permission of *Ladies' Home Journal.* © 1964 by The Curtis Publishing Company.

DUVALL, EVELYN M. and SYLVANUS M. *Sense and Nonsense about Sex.* New York: Association Press, 1962.

EHRMANN, WINSTON W. *Premarital Dating Behavior.* New York: Henry Holt and Company, Inc., 1959.

FORD, CLELLAN S., and BEACH, FRANK A. *Patterns of Sexual Behavior.* New York: Harper & Brothers, 1951, p. 307.

GOLDING, WILLIAM. *Lord of the Flies.* New York: Coward-McCann, Inc., 1954.

KINSEY, ALFRED C., *et al. Sexual Behavior in the Human Female.* Philadelphia: W. B. Saunders Co., 1953.

———. *Sexual Behavior in the Human Male.* Philadelphia: W. B. Saunders Co., 1948.

KIRKENDALL, LESTER A. "Physical and Mental Health Implications of Sex Beliefs and Practices among Adolescents." Unpublished paper distributed at the Groves Conference on Marriage and the Family, St. Louis, April 30, 1963.

PEALE, NORMAN VINCENT. "What's Happening to Sex in America?" *Guideposts,* July, 1964, pp. 2–6.

SALINGER, J. D. *The Catcher in the Rye.* Boston: Little, Brown & Company, 1951.

CHAPTER 4—It's Fun—Always?

BURGESS, ERNEST W., and WALLIN, PAUL. *Engagement and Marriage.* Philadelphia: J. B. Lippincott Co., 1953, Chapter 12, "Assessing Premarital Intercourse."

CHRISTENSEN, HAROLD T., and CARPENTER, GEORGE R. "Value-Behavior Discrepancies Regarding Premarital Coitus in Three Western Cultures." *American Sociological Review,* XXVII, No. 1 (February, 1962), pp. 66–74.

CLARK, LEMON. "Marriage, Sexual Adjustment in." Reprinted from *The Encyclopedia of Sexual Behavior,* Albert Ellis and Albert Abarbanel, eds. New York: Hawthorn Books, Inc., 1961, pp. 710–717.

DAVIDSON, ROBERT F. *Philosophies Men Live By.* New York: The Dryden Press, 1952, p. 53.

DESCHIN, CELIA S. *Teen-Agers and Venereal Disease.* Washington, D.C.: U.S. Department of Health, Education, and Welfare, Public Health Service, 1961, p. 59.

DUNBAR, FLANDERS. *Your Teenager's Mind and Body.* New York: Hawthorn Books, Inc., 1962, p. 253.

EHRMANN, WINSTON W. *Premarital Dating Behavior.* New York: Henry Holt and Company, Inc., 1959.

KINSEY, ALFRED C., *et al. Sexual Behavior in the Human Female.* Philadelphia: W. B. Saunders Co., 1953.

KIRKENDALL, LESTER A. "Sex Education of Adolescents: An Exchange—Values and Premarital Intercourse—Implications for Parent Education." *Marriage and Family Living,* XXII, No. 4 (November, 1960), pp. 317–322.

KIRKPATRICK, CLIFFORD. *The Family as Process and Institution.* New York: The Ronald Press Company, 2nd ed., 1963, Chapter 14, "Youth and Sex Expression," pp. 346–374.

LYND, HELEN MERRILL. *On Shame and the Search for Identity.* New York: Harcourt-Brace, 1958.

MERYMAN, RICHARD. "Marilyn Lets Her Hair Down about Being Famous." *Life,* August 3, 1962.

PRIESTLEY, J. B. "Eroticism, Sex and Love." *The Saturday Evening Post,* April 27, 1963.

SCHAUFFLER, GOODRICH C., M.D. "Today It Could Be *Your* Daughter." *Ladies' Home Journal,* January, 1958.

"Tragedy of Marilyn: Unclaimed in Death." Associated Press report, August 6, 1962.

WALTERS, PAUL A. "Sex and the College Woman." Report of Address at the American Orthopsychiatric Association Meeting. *Chicago Daily News,* March 21, 1964, p. 17.

CHAPTER 5—If You Are Really in Love—Why Not?

BLOOD, ROBERT O., JR. "Romance and Premarital Intercourse—Incompatibles?" *Marriage and Family Living,* XIV, No. 2 (May, 1952), pp. 105–108.

BURGESS, ERNEST W., and WALLIN, PAUL. *Engagement and Marriage.* Philadelphia: J. B. Lippincott Co., 1953, Chapter 12, "Assessing Premarital Intercourse," pp. 353–390.

DUVALL, EVELYN MILLIS. *Love and the Facts of Life.* New York: Association Press, 1963, Part One, "Your Love Feelings," pp. 14–74.

DUVALL, EVELYN M. and SYLVANUS M. *Sense and Nonsense About Sex.* New York: Association Press, 1962, Chapter 5, "Love Is Not the Same as Sex," pp. 72–89.

EHRMANN, WINSTON W. *Premarital Dating Behavior.* New York: Henry Holt and Company, Inc., 1959.

ERIKSON, ERIK H. *Childhood and Society.* New York: W. W. Norton & Company, Inc., 1950.

FROMM, ERICH. *The Art of Loving.* New York: Harper & Brothers, 1956.

KINSEY, ALFRED C., et al. *Sexual Behavior in the Human Female.* Philadelphia: W. B. Saunders Co., 1953, Chapter 8, "Pre-Marital Coitus," pp. 282–345.

———. *Sexual Behavior in the Human Male.* Philadelphia: W. B. Saunders Co., 1948, Chapter 17, "Pre-Marital Intercourse," pp. 547–562.

KIRKPATRICK, CLIFFORD. *The Family as Process and Institution.* New York: The Ronald Press Company, rev. ed., 1963, Chapter 14, "Youth and Sex Expression," pp. 346–374.

LANDIS, JUDSON T. "Adjustments After Marriage." *Marriage and Family Living,* IX, No. 2 (May, 1947), pp. 32–34.

PRIESTLEY, J. B. "Eroticism, Sex and Love." *The Saturday Evening Post,* April 27, 1963, pp. 10 and 14.

REIK, THEODOR. *The Psychology of Sex Relations.* New York: Rinehart, 1945, p. 124.

REISS, IRA L. *Premarital Sexual Standards in America.* Glencoe, Illinois: The Free Press, 1960, p. 251.

SHIPMAN, GORDON. "Attitudes of College Students Toward Premarital Sex Experience." Unpublished data of a study reported in *The Coordinator,* 1958.

WALLER, WILLARD, and HILL, REUBEN. *The Family: A Dynamic Interpretation.* New York: The Dryden Press, 1958, p. 198.

CHAPTER 6—Is Sexual Restraint Bad for You?

American Institute of Family Relations, The. "Premarital Experience No Help in Sexual Adjustment after Marriage." *Family Life,* XXI, No. 8 (August, 1961), pp. 1, 2.

Association of State and Territorial Health Officers, The; American Venereal Disease Association, The; American Social Health Association, The. *Today's VD Control Problem: A Joint Statement.* The American Social Health Association, March, 1963.

BINGER, CARL, M.D. "The Pressures on College Girls Today." *The Atlantic Monthly,* February, 1961, pp. 40–44.

BROWN, WILLIAM J., M.D. "Venereal Disease Education Can't Wait." Address delivered at the VD Conference, Chicago, Illinois, November 9, 1962, mimeographed paper.

BURGESS, ERNEST W., and WALLIN, PAUL. *Engagement and Marriage.* Philadelphia: J. B. Lippincott Co., 1953, p. 372.

CALDERONE, MARY STEICHEN, M.D. "A Distinguished Doctor Talks to Vassar College Freshmen about Love and Sex." *Redbook,* February, 1964, pp. 39, 114–118.

DESCHIN, CELIA S. *Teen-Agers and Venereal Disease: A Sociological Study.* Atlanta: Venereal Disease Branch, U. S. Department of Health, Education, and Welfare, 1961, 168 pp.

————. "Teenagers and Venereal Disease." *Children,* July–August, 1962.

DRESKIN, NATHAN. "The Unwed Father." *Canadian Weekly (Toronto Star),* February 9–14, 1964.

Gallup Poll, "Number of U. S. Drinkers Up Sharply Over Last 5 Years." Syndicated feature, February 5, 1964.

HILLIARD, MARION, M.D. "Why Premarital Sex Is Always Wrong." *Ladies' Home Journal,* September, 1958, p. 161.

KANIN, EUGENE J. "Premarital Sex Adjustments, Social Class, and Associated Behaviors." *Marriage and Family Living,* XXII, No. 3 (August, 1960), pp. 258–262.

KINSEY, ALFRED C., *et al. Sexual Behavior in the Human Female.* Philadelphia: W. B. Saunders Co., 1953, p. 329.

KIRKPATRICK, CLIFFORD. *What Science Says About Happiness in Marriage.* Minneapolis: Burgess Publishing Co., 1947, p. 24.

LEIGHTON, DOROTHEA C., and associates. *The Character of Danger,* Vol. III. New York: Basic Books, 1963, 545 pp.

LOCKE, HARVEY. *Predicting Adjustment in Marriage: A Comparison of a Divorced and a Happily Married Group.* New York: Henry Holt and Company, Inc., 1951, p. 134.

RUTTER, RICHARD. "Cigarette Sales Are Rebounding." *The New York Times,* March 15, 1964, Section 3, pp. 1, 14.

SCHWARTZ, WILLIAM F. "Some Pragmatic Considerations in Venereal Disease Education." Address Delivered at American Public Health Association, Miami Beach, Florida, October 18, 1962, mimeographed paper.

TERMAN, LEWIS M., *et al. Psychological Factors in Marital Happiness.* New York: McGraw-Hill Book Company, 1938, p. 325.

THOMAS, EVAN W. "Venereal Disease Information for Health Educators, Nurses and Discussion Leaders." Address delivered March 12, 1963, mimeographed paper.

TYLER, RALPH W. "Pressure Points in the Crucial Years." Address prepared for the VD Conference, Chicago, Illinois, 1962, mimeographed paper.

CHAPTER 7—Is Pregnancy a Possibility?

ALLEN, MARY LOUISE. "What Can We Do about America's Unwed Teen-Age Mothers?" *McCall's,* November, 1963, pp. 40, 42, 51, 214.

CHRISTENSEN, HAROLD T. "Child Spacing Analysis Via Record Linkage: New Data Plus a Summing Up from Earlier Reports." *Marriage and Family Living,* XXV, No. 3 (August, 1963), pp. 272–280.

————. "Studies in Child Spacing: I—Premarital Pregnancy as Measured by the Spacing of the First Birth to Marriage." *American Sociological Review,* XVIII, No. 1 (February, 1953), pp. 53–59.

————; ANDREWS, ROBERT; and FREISER, SOPHIE. "Falsification of Age at Marriage." *Marriage and Family Living,* XV, No. 4 (November, 1953), pp. 301–304.

CHRISTENSEN, CORNELIA V., M.D. "Premarital Pregnancies and Their Outcome." *Journal of the National Association of Women Deans and Counselors,* XXVI, No. 2 (January, 1963), pp. 29–33.

DAMON, VIRGIL G., M.D., and TAVES, ISABELLA. "My Daughter Is in Trouble." *Look,* August 14, 1962.

DAVIDSON, MURIEL. "The Deadly Favor." *Ladies' Home Journal,* November, 1963, pp. 53–57.

GALLAGHER, URSULA M. "What of the Unmarried Parent?" *Journal of Home Economics,* LV, No. 6 (June, 1963), pp. 401–405.

GEBHARD, P. H.; POMEROY, W. B.; MARTIN, C. E.; and CHRISTENSEN, C. V. *Pregnancy, Birth and Abortion.* New York: Harper-Hoeber, 1958.

GUTTMACHER, ALAN F., M.D. *Babies by Choice or by Chance.* New York: Doubleday & Company, Inc., 1959.

Handbook on Sex Instruction in Swedish Schools. Stockholm, Sweden: Royal Board of Education, 1957, p. 8.

KIRKENDALL, LESTER A. "Sex Education of Adolescents: An Exchange—Values and Premarital Intercourse—Implications for Parent Education." *Marriage and Family Living,* XXII, No. 4 (November, 1960), pp. 317–322.

KOTULAK, RONALD. " 'You Keep Baby,' Mothers Tell Hospital." *Chicago Tribune,* April 12, 1964.

LANDIS, JUDSON T., and POFFENBERGER, THOMAS and SHIRLEY. "The Effects of First Pregnancy upon the Sexual Adjustment of 212 Couples." *American Sociological Review,* XV, No. 6 (December, 1950), pp. 767–772.

McHUGH, GELOLO. "10,000 Interviews Reveal What People Don't Know about Sex Fact and Fiction." *True Story* (February, 1961), pp. 40, 41, 117, 118, 119.

PANNOR, REUBEN. "Casework Service for Unmarried Fathers." *Children,* X, No. 2 (March–April, 1963), pp. 65–70. By permission of the author.

"Pills, The: More Effective, and More of Them." *Time,* March 20, 1964, p. 64.

RINEHART, JONATHAN. "Mothers without Joy." *The Saturday Evening Post,* March 23, 1963, pp. 29–30.

ROCK, JOHN, M.D. *The Time Has Come.* New York: Avon Books, 1963.

VINCENT, CLARK. *Unmarried Mothers.* New York: The Free Press, 1961.

CHAPTER 8—Would You Like to Live Where Sex Is Easy?

BLOOD, ROBERT O., JR. "Romance and Premarital Intercourse—Incompatibles?" *Marriage and Family Living,* XIV, No. 2 (May, 1952), pp. 105–108.

CHRISTENSEN, HAROLD T. "Premarital Sex Norms in America and Scandinavia." *Journal of the National Association of Women Deans and Counselors,* XXVI, No. 2 (January, 1963), pp. 16–21.

———. "Timing of First Pregnancy as a Factor in Divorce: A Cross-Cultural Analysis." *Eugenics Quarterly,* X, No. 3 (September, 1963), pp. 119–130.

"Despite Church's Protest, Danes Get TV Sex Lecture." Associated Press release, Copenhagen, March 21, 1964.

FORD, CLELLEN S., and BEACH, FRANK A. *Patterns of Sexual Behavior.* New York: Harper & Brothers, 1951.

Handbook on Sex Instruction in Swedish Schools. Stockholm, Sweden: Royal Board of Education, 1957.

HENDIN, HERBERT. *Suicide and Scandinavia.* New York: Grune & Stratton, Inc., 1964.

HOFFMEYER, HENRIK, M.D. Unpublished address at the Groves Conference on Marriage and the Family, St. Louis, Missouri, April 29, 1963.

LEWIS, C. S. "We Have No 'Right to Happiness.' " *The Saturday Evening Post,* December 21–28, 1963, pp. 10, 12.

LINTON, RALPH. *The Study of Man.* New York: Appleton-Century-Crofts, 1936.

MALINOWSKI, BRONISLAW. *The Sexual Life of Savages in North-West Melanesia.* London: Routledge, 1929.

MEAD, MARGARET. *Coming of Age in Samoa.* New York: Blue Ribbon Books, 1928.

METCALFE, ROBERT. "Abortion Rate Alarms Japan." United Press International release, Tokyo, September 29, 1963.

REIK, THEODOR. *The Psychology of Sex Relations.* New York: Rinehart, 1945.

REISS, IRA L. "The Scaling of Premarital Sexual Permissiveness." *Journal of Marriage and the Family,* XXVI, No. 2 (May, 1964), pp. 188-198.

SPOCK, BENJAMIN. "Psychology Can't Substitute for Morality." *Redbook,* January, 1964, pp. 22, 24, 25.

TOUSSIENG, POVL W., M.D. Personal communication dated October 8, 1964.

CHAPTER 9—Religion—How Important Is It?

BAILEY, DERRICK SHERWIN. *Sexual Relations in Christian Thought.* New York: Harper & Brothers, 1959.

BURGESS, ERNEST W., and WALLIN, PAUL. *Engagement and Marriage.* Philadelphia: J. B. Lippincott Co., 1953, pp. 338-346.

DESCHIN, CELIA S. *Teen-Agers and Venereal Disease*. Atlanta, Georgia: U. S. Department of Health, Education, and Welfare, Venereal Disease Branch, pp. 93–94.

DUVALL, EVELYN M. and SYLVANUS M. *Sense and Nonsense About Sex*. New York: Association Press, 1962.

DUVALL, SYLVANUS M. *Men, Women, and Morals*. New York: Association Press, 1952.

FEUCHT, OSCAR E., ed. *Sex and the Church*. St. Louis, Missouri: Concordia Publishing House, 1961.

JOSSELYN, IRENE, M.D. "Some Reflections on Adolescent Rebellion." *Children*, XI, No. 3 (May–June, 1964), pp. 122-123.

KINSEY, ALFRED C., et al. *Sexual Behavior in the Human Female*. Philadelphia: W. B. Saunders Co., 1953, pp. 304, 318, 319, 331, 344.

KLEMER, RICHARD H. "Student Attitudes toward Guidance in Sexual Morality." *Marriage and Family Living*, XXIV, No. 3 (August, 1962), pp. 260-264.

LIEBMAN, JOSHUA LOTH. *Peace of Mind*. New York: Simon and Schuster, Inc., 1946, 203 pp.

MENEILLY, ROBERT H. "The Sex Drive, Gift of God." *The Christian Athlete*, VI, No. 9 (October–November, 1963), pp. 10-12.

PORTER, BLAINE M. "Critique on Symposium of Reiss, Stokes and Poffenberger Papers." *Marriage and Family Living*, XXIV, No. 3 (August, 1962), pp. 274–277.

Report of a Consultation on the Changing Relationships of Men and Women in Church, Family and Society. New York: National Council of Churches, 1963.

"Sex in the Student Perspective." *The Intercollegian*, LXXXI, No. 6 (April, 1964), entire issue.

SPOCK, BENJAMIN, M.D. "How Parents Can Help Adolescents Understand Sex." *Ladies' Home Journal*, April, 1962.

THOMAS, JOHN L. *The American Catholic Family*. Englewood Cliffs, New Jersey: Prentice-Hall, Inc., 1956.

CHAPTER 10—How Does It Affect Your Marriage, Your Family?

BEALER, ROBERT C.; WILLITS, FERN K.; and MAIDA, PETER R. "The Rebellious Youth Subculture—a Myth." *Children* (March–April, 1964), pp. 43–48.

BURGESS, ERNEST W., and WALLIN, PAUL. *Engagement and Marriage*. Philadelphia: J. B. Lippincott Co., 1953, Chapter 12.

CHRISTENSEN, HAROLD T., and MEISSNER, HANNA H. "Premarital Pregnancy as a Factor in Divorce." *American Sociological Review*, XVIII, No. 6 (December, 1953), pp. 631–644.

COLEMAN, JAMES S. *The Adolescent Society*. New York: The Free Press, 1961.

DUVALL, EVELYN MILLIS. "Young Moderns' Marriage Dreams." *The PTA Magazine*, April, 1963, pp. 4–7.

DUVALL, SYLVANUS M. "Facts and Fictions about Sex." *Look*, April 12, 1960.

HARRIS, DALE B., and TSENG, SING CHU. "Children's Attitudes toward Peers and Parents as Revealed by Sentence Completions." *Child Development*, December, 1957.

HENTON, JUNE MARCUM. "The Effects of Married High School Students on their Unmarried Classmates." *Journal of Marriage and the Family*, XXVI, No. 1 (February, 1964), pp. 87–88.

HESS, ROBERT D., and GOLDBLATT, IRENE. "The Status of Adolescents in American Society: a Problem in Social Identity." *Child Development*, December, 1957.

HULME, WILLIAM E. *God, Sex and Youth*. Englewood Cliffs, New Jersey: Prentice-Hall, Inc., 1959, p. 120.

KELLY, E. LOWELL. "The Re-assessment of Specific Attitudes after Twenty Years." *The Journal of Social Issues*, XVII, No. 1 (1961), pp. 29–37.

KIRKPATRICK, CLIFFORD. *The Family as Process and Institution*. New York: The Ronald Press, 2nd ed., 1963, pp. 354–355.

LEES, HANNAH. "Why Husbands Stay Faithful." *Redbook*, July, 1962, pp. 33, 85–87.

LOCKE, HARVEY J. *Predicting Adjustment in Marriage*. New York: Henry Holt and Company, Inc., 1951, p. 133.

MACE, DAVID R. "Is Chastity Outmoded?" *Women's Home Companion*, September, 1949, pp. 37, 38, 101.

RIEMER, GEORGE. "A Frank Look at Marital Fidelity." *Good Housekeeping*, January, 1964, pp. 49, 141, 142.

SAXE, LOUIS P., M.D. *Sex and the Mature Man*. New York: Gilbert Press and Julian Messner, Inc., 1964.

TERMAN, LEWIS M., *et al. Psychological Factors in Marital Happiness*. New York: McGraw-Hill Book Company, 1938, pp. 326, 340.

WILSON, PAUL B., and BUCK, ROY C. "Pennsylvania's Rural Youth Express their Opinions." Pennsylvania Agricultural Experiment Station Progress Report No. 134, 1955.

WINTER, GIBSON. *Love and Conflict: New Patterns in Family Life*. Garden City, New York: Doubleday & Company, Inc., 1958, p. 27.

CHAPTER 11—What Happens to Your Reputation?

BENJAMIN, HERBERT S., M.D. "What Is a Young Adult?" *Coronet*, October, 1958, pp. 78–82.

BERTOCCI, PETER A. *Religion as Creative Insecurity*. New York: Association Press, 1958, 128 pp.

HORNEY, KAREN, M.D. *Our Inner Conflicts*. New York: W. W. Norton & Company, Inc., 1945, 250 pp.

JOHNSON, KATHRYN. "Girls Need Egos Restored." Associated Press release, March 19, 1964.

KIRKENDALL, LESTER A. "Sex and Social Policy." *Clinical Pediatrics*, III, No. 4 (April, 1964), pp. 236–246.

LEVY, ALAN. "Two Years Have Passed Since Charles Van Doren Confessed His Part in the Television Scandal." *Redbook*, November, 1961, pp. 43, 126–131.

LIEBMAN, JOSHUA LOTH. *Peace of Mind*. New York: Simon and Schuster, Inc., 1946, 203 pp.

STIRLING, REBECCA BIRCH. "Some Psychological Mechanisms Operative in Gossip." *Social Forces*, XXXIV, No. 3 (March, 1956), pp. 262–267.

CHAPTER 12—How Do You See Yourself?

CRAIG, MAY. "A Woman Writer Speaks Up." Portland, Maine, *Sunday Telegram*, February 9, 1964.

DOUVAN, ELIZABETH, and KAYE, CAROL. "Motivational Factors in College Entrance." Nevitt Sanford, ed. *The American College*. New York: John Wiley & Sons, Inc., 1962, pp. 199–224.

DUVALL, EVELYN MILLIS. "Adolescent Love as a Reflection of Teen-Agers' Search for Identity." *Journal of Marriage and the Family*, XXVI, No. 2 (May, 1964), pp. 226–229.

———. *Love and the Facts of Life*. New York: Association Press, 1963.

EPSTEIN, N. B., M.D. "Inner Life of the Family." Address delivered at the Canadian Conference on the Family, June, 1964, mimeographed.

ERIKSON, ERIK H. *Childhood and Society*. New York: W. W. Norton & Company, Inc., 1950, pp. 229–231.

FREUD, SIGMUND. *New Introductory Lectures on Psychoanalysis*. New York: W. W. Norton & Company, Inc., 1933, p. 17.

HIMELHOCH, JEROME. "Sex Education in Sociological Perspective." *Social Hygiene Papers*, November, 1957.

HUNT, MORTON, and CORMAN, RENA. "The Tormented Generation." *The Saturday Evening Post*, October 12, 1963, pp. 30–34.

KIRKENDALL, LESTER A. "The Problems of Remaining a Virgin." Reprinted from *Sexology*, p. 602.

LEUBA, CLARENCE. *Ethics in Sex Conduct*. New York: Association Press, 1948, 164 pp.

LOEB, MARTIN B. "Social Role and Sexual Identity in Adolescent Males." Address to National Association of Social Workers, 1959.

LUNN, ARNOLD, and LEAN, GARTH. *The New Morality*. London: Blandford Press, 1964, 154 pp.

LYND, HELEN MERRILL. *On Shame and the Search for Identity*. New York: Harcourt-Brace, 1958.

SPENDER, STEPHEN. *World within World*. London: Hamish Hamilton, 1951, pp. 9–10.

STRAUSS, ANSELM L. *Mirrors and Masks: The Search for Identity*. New York: The Free Press, 1959.

UNWIN, J. D. *Sex and Culture*. Oxford, England: Oxford University Press, 1934.

Index